Investors' Protection

A Study on Legal Aspects

Investors' Protection

A Study on Legal Aspects

Dr. R. Neelamegam
Dr. R. Srinivasan
(M.A. Corp.; M.Phil Corp., M.Com; Ph.D Corporate)
Lecturer, Deptt. of Corporate Secretaryship
Bharathidasan Govt College for Women
Pondicherry - 3

RAJ PUBLICATIONS
DELHI-110009

Investors' Protection : A Study on Legal Aspects

Published by :
Smt. Poonam Goel
for **Raj Publications**
R-115/2 Model Town-III
Delhi-110009
Phone-7466486
Fax-011-3557717

ISBN-81-86208-08-9

1998

Laser Typesetting by:
Aarati Computers
F-11/12, Model Town, Delhi-9
Ph. 7240075

Printed in India

Contents

Preface

In recent years, capital market has emerged as a major source of finance for the Indian corporate sector, with the primary market having been accessed to the tune of over Rs. 22,000 cores in the year 1994. In the secondary market, with 23 recognised stock exchanges operating in the country, the number of listed companies thereon, their daily turnover, the market capitalisation and so forth, have increased tramendously, also witnessing in the process a rapid enlargement of the investor population to around 40 millions.

The investor grienvances and complaints thereof have increased even after the establishment of the SEBI. The number of complaints which were resolved has, of course, increased recently. Over 60,000 investor grievances were reported to have been resolved, after the SEBI referred them to above 4,000 companies during the first half of August 1997. Amid this background, the present book titled 'Investors' Protection' has assumed greater significance than ever before. The book is first of its kind in the field in giving a detailed account on the effectiveness/lapses of existing statutes meant for investor protection. The salient feature is practical suggestions for investor protection offered by the stock brokers, investors and exports in the field are in corporated in the book. The book serves as a valuable guide to any body interested in capital market and investment.

I would be failing in my duty if I had not conveyed my special thanks to M/s Raj Publications, Delhi for their sincere effort in bringing out this book in time.

— Dr. R. Neelamegam
— Dr. R. Srinivasan

1

Introduction and Design of the Study

Stock exchanges of the country have not been able to deal effectively with the grievances of the investor public for the reason that they are like clubs of member-brokers, established by the members-brokers for the benefit of their members. The paramount interest of the exchanges appears to be to safeguard the personal and pecuniary interest of members and not to solve the problems of the investors, notwithstanding fresh winds blowing into the exchanges.

With the multiplicity of authorities, and the grievances of investors mounting, there is not much hope left for the investor in the present environment, besides the SEBI, the stock exchangers and the Department of Company Affairs, the investor' service center in private sector duly recognised by the central government should also come out in adequate number. Such centers vested with appropriate power may be established to look with sympathy and understanding of the investors' problems. These centres may have the task to take effective and prompt actions and also have an exclusive jurisdiction to deal with the woes of the investors.

In this regard, it is worthwhile to mention that the year 1992-a special year for the stock markets in India. That is when the rot of securities scandal set in on April 2, 1992, the Bombay Stock Exchange (BSE) sensex (30-scrip index) scaled the peak–an all-time high-at 4546.58 points-an abnormal boom. After the big scam ripped open the secret deals of the stock and securities realm in India, the index crashed down to its bench-mark level, 2000 points in mid 1993. The period in between withered a lot of dramatic statements, declaration, findings, and so forth. The final report of Janakiraman Committee put the gross amount involved in the irregular transactions, circumventing the Reserve Bank of India's (RBI) regulations as Rs. 4,024.45 crores. With the RBI and the SEBI stepping-in with more controls and regulations, the rot seemed to have been contained. But, the incident drilled many a deep hole in the pockets of small investors, and leaving an indelible mark-rather a stain on the so-called regulatory bodies, which failed to protect the investing community in India.

Statement of the Problem

In India, in the context of the share markets witnessed of stock market scam, it is now clear that there must be a closer regulation of the share markets and thereby giving protection to the investors become necessary in the legislations concerned. For instance, SEBI's Act 1992, had been put more teeth into it, authority was complete for doing a job of regulation that companies should set up an investors' redressal cell across the country to look after the investors' complaints such as non receipt of share certificates sent for transfer, share split up, endorsements, non receipt of bonus shares, rights issue, dividends and so forth.

In addition to the above, the stock markets all over the country with the securities scam had also its own harmful effect on the share markets scaring away investors' who had seen only the bright side of the operations. But now the investors' confidence hit the rock bottom and remained low for a long time, the problem was basically lack of transparency in dealings between the broker and the investor. This type of problem will not arise if the regulatory bodies are given adequate power to contain speculation and take corrective measures whenever market has been going for purchase and sale of securities. It should be emphasised that it would be necessary to regulate the stock markets, because stock exchangs are the citadel of captial and the temple of values. The dealings in the stock market must be corrected, which is the only way to avoid excessive gains made by the brokers, top managements of companies and to protect the innocent investors' from cheating. The present study analyses the problems faced by the investors of corporate securities and attempts to offer concrete solutions to tackle such problems.

Objectives of the Study

The objectives set out below prompted to undertake the study under report:–

1. To study the avenues available to the investing community and need for investors' protection.
2. To examine the adequacy of various protective measures offered under the existing Companies Act, 1956, Securities Contracts (Regulation) Act, 1956, and SEBI Act 1992 for investors' protection.
3. To examine the on going trading activities both in the primary market and secondary market in India.
4. To survey the opinions of experts in stock market trading with regard to the extent of adequacy of the statutory measures meant for protecting the interest of investors from the undesirable dealings in stock markets.
5. To study the functioning of investors' service undertakings in India.
6. To find out the problems of the investors and to offer concrete suggestions for redressing the grievances of the investing community.

Selection of the Topic

In the recent past, security markets have become dynamic and now one can see that there is a sea of change in the share market front. The number of investors investing in shares and other securities has shot up tremendously, hence INVESTORS' PROTECTION has become a burning issue. The recent developments in the stock markets have created such an amazing popularity and awareness among the public about the new avenues of investments, healthy trade practices, investors' protection and role of the stock exchanges. The introduction of modified 'Badla' trading, increasing insider trading practices, the problem of price fixation, and SEBI's role in investors' protection have necessitated a study on the important factors governing the primary and the secondary markets and the legal aspects in investors' protection; Hence the present study titled "INVESTORS' PROTECTION, A STUDY ON LEGAL ASPECTS".

Importance of the Study

The introduction of modified "Badla" trading, confusion over price fixation and the like–the aftermaths of the securities market scandal, the demand for investors' protection had been justified. There is an increasing interest among the stock market circles and the public to know the views of stock brokers, investors' and professionals, and the persons connected with the stock market on stock market trading activities. The present study examines the opinions of these respondents who have a knowledge on the present burning issues like insider trading, pricing of securities, badla system, futures and options and investors' protection.

Some of the studies were conducted earlier and that too on investors' behaviour. The present study makes a pioneering attempt on analysing the effectiveness or otherwise of the statutory framework meant for investors' protection. Therefore, this study might stand in good stead to understand the background, views of stock brokers, professionals and investors in the field and various measures to be taken to protect the interests of investors.

Scope of the Study

1. The present study throws light on the problems of investors' especially in Tamilnadu State, and therefore the sample survey is mainly confined to the geographical area in and around Madras city.

2. The reference period of the study was for three years, namely, from June 1992-93 to July 1995.

Figure 1.1 shows the location of metropolitan city, Madras, in Tamilnadu State (India).

Figure 1.1

Location of Metropolitan City, Madras in Tamilnadu State

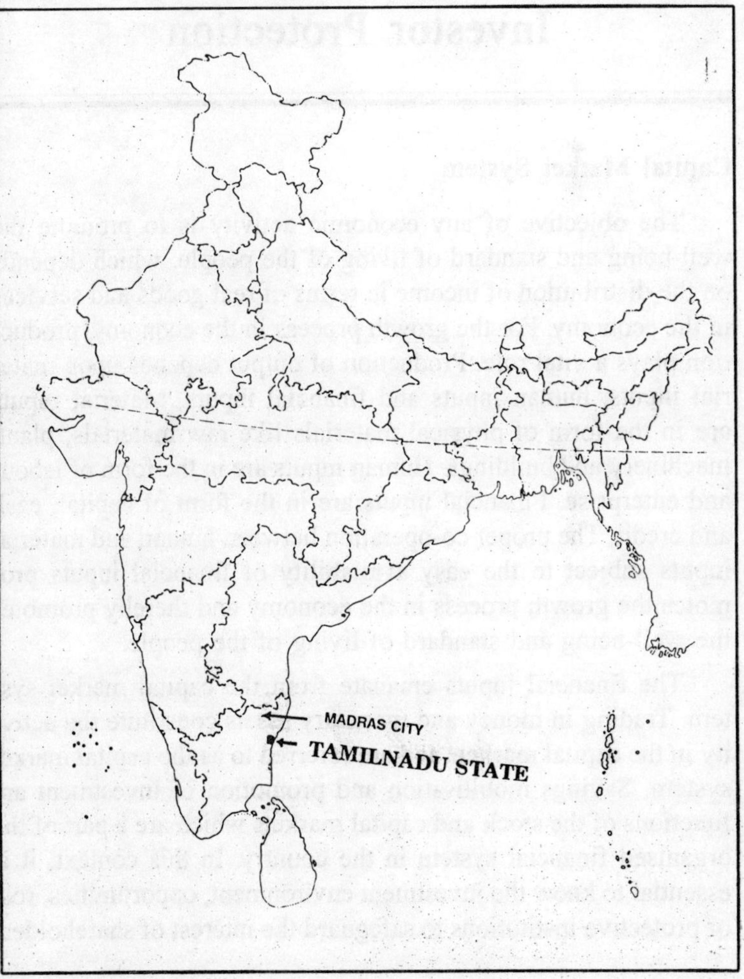

2

Investment Environment and Investor Protection

Capital Market System

The objective of any economic activity is to promote the well-being and standard of living of the people, which depends on the distribution of income in terms of real goods and services in the economy. For the growth process in the economy, production plays a vital role. Production of output depends upon material inputs, human inputs and financial inputs. Material inputs are in the form of physical materials like raw materials, plant, machinery and buildings. Human inputs are in the form of labour and enterprise. Financial inputs are in the form of capital, cash and credit. The proper co-operation between human and material inputs subject to the easy availability of financial inputs promotes the growth process in the economy and thereby promotes the well-being and standard of living of the people.

The financial inputs emanate from the capital market system. Trading in money and monetary assets constitute the activity in the capital markets and are referred to as the capital market system. Savings mobilisation and promotion of investment are functions of the stock and capital markets which are a part of the organised financial system in the country. In this context, it is essential to know the investment environment, opportunities, role of protective institutions to safeguard the interest of shareholders and debentureholders. This has been highlighted in the following passages of this chapter.

Stock and Capital Market

The term 'Capital Market" is used in the wider sense as to include both the new issues market and the stock market[1]. In this sense, both primary and secondary markets are covered here. The trading in the stock market is debt claims of a medium and long-terms nature which can be classified into those of the Government sector and of the private sector. The securities of government are traded in the stock market as a separate component, called gilt-edged market. These securities include those of the Central and State Governments, local bodies, semi-government bodies and those guaranteed by the Government. In this market, there are again three types of securities–short, medium and long-dated Government securities, depending on the maturity period. Another component of the stock market deals with trading in corporate securities such as equity shares, preference shares and debentures. Equities are shares of companies of the ownership category. When these equities are floated to the public for the first time by the companies as shares, they constitute the new issues market , which is a component of the capital market and when the same securities are traded again and again as secondary items, they constitute secondary markets.

Primary or New Issue Market

The new issue market deals with the raising of fresh capital either for cash or for consideration other than cash by companies and encompasses all institutions dealing in the issue of fresh claims. The forms in which these claims are incurred are equity shares, preference shares, debentures, rights, bonds, deposits, miscellaneous loans and so forth. All the financial institutions in the capital market which contribute, underwrite or directly subscribe are part of the new issue market.

Initial issues are those floated by new companies for the first time, while further issues are subsequent issues floated by the existing companies. Capital issues can also be classified as those given for cash, for exchange of technical know-how, exchange of shares of another company or exchange for any other services rendered by the agencies or promoters. The placement of the issues may be through (a) prospectus (b) offer of sale (c) private placement and (d) rights issue.

Secondary Market

Already issued and listed securities are traded in the secondary stock market. Shares, debentures and other securities are trade in the stock market. Money flows in daily through the trading of these securities. Secondary market is one of the main segments of financial system of the country. Securities Contracts (Regulation) Act, 1956, regulates the stock exchanges in the country.

Investment Environment

The investment environment in India is easily the most congenial for individual investors. The capital market is fairly well-organised and growing fast too. There are government sponsored investment schemes, as well as private sector sponsored investment schemes, representing the true options of a mixed economy.

First of all, the way through which an individual investor makes his investment can be classified into (I) Direct Investment and (II) Indirect Investment. A brief explanation of these two types is given below:–

I. Direct Investment

Under this, the investors directly participate in the investment process.

They analyse the investment opportunities, select and manage.

Example: Investing in common stock, preferred stock, bonds and real estate.

II. Indirect Investment

Here, the investor invests through investment companies and

mutual funds. The saving accounts and other bank deposits are termed voluntary indirect investments wherein the deposits are utilised for further investments.

Recent Government's Policies of Liberalisation and SEBI Guidelines for Investor Protection

The Capital Issues (Control) Act 1947 which controlled the issue of capital was repealed on 29th May 1992. In View of this, issue of capital by companies has been freed from the requirements of approval from the Controller of Capital Issues (CCI). With a view to ensuring disclosure and investor protection, SEBI issued guidelines on 11th June, 1992 for compliance by the companies making capital issue[2]. The guidelines issued by SEBI are as follows:–

A new company without a track record is permitted to issue capital to public only at par. But new companies set up by existing companies with a five year track record of consistent profitability will be free to price its issue provided the participation of the promoting companies is not less than 50% of equity of the new company and the issue price is made applicable to all investors uniformly including promoters.

First issues by existing private closely held companies with a three year track record of consistent profitability are permitted to freely price the issue and list their securities on the stock exchange provided that (a) not less than 20% of the equity offered for subscription by public (b) the draft prospectus is vetted by SEBI (c) the pricing is determined both by the issues and the lead managers to issue. Such companies are obligated to disclose its net assets value as per the last audited Balance Sheet and justification for the issue price in the issue documents.

Existing listed companies are allowed to raise fresh capital by freely pricing their further issues. These companies too have to disclose net assets value; further, high and low price of the shares for the last two years should be disclosed in the prospectus, which will be vetted by SEBI.

Underwriting is now mandatory for the issue of capital to the public.

It has been stipulated by SEBI that companies issuing new financial instruments, whether by way of rights or otherwise should make adequate disclosure regarding the terms and conditions, redemption, security, conversion and other relevant features of the instruments and the disclosure. It should be vetted by SEBI.

The guidelines state that in case of issue where application and allotment money aggregating Rs. 250 crores and above are raised, the issues should disclose and make arrangements for the use of proceeds of the issue and funds so raised will be monitored by one of the financial institutions. It has also included some additional conditions on bonus issue. It states that bonus issue should not be made within 12 months of any rights public issue. For the protection of the interest of the debentureholders, it provides some guidelines.

Thus under the new environment, funds will not easily flow in for projects being set up by companies till they convince shareholders of their viability. Shareholders will not readily accept full promises made casually by managements on the eve of floatation of equity issue or convertible debentures.

But still there is a large scope for manipulation. Any survey of public issue by existing companies in the past will show that share prices start raising week or even months before the date of new issue. Very often, these price shoot ups are part of an exercise to rig the market and obtain high premium on the new issues of capital.

But SEBI has suggested guidelines to plug these loopholes. It has not only suggested that there should be full underwriting by atleast three banks of every existing companies fresh issue of capital but has also attempted to make the underwriters accountable to issues, the principal underwriters would have to provide a safety net for investors for a certain period of time after the closure of the issue, when they should be prepared to buy back the shares from the original investors upto their limits of underwriting, in case the market price falls below 20- 40% of the issue price depending on the extent of premium.[3]

Another manipulation by companies is the non disclosure of adequate information though SEBI is insisting on the companies for proper revealing of details. Companies give detailed report to foreign investors but such information is not provided to local investors.

The general view is that, the SEBIs guidelines do not provide a cover for small investors. It should have been more unambigously defined the terms, like manipulation or rigging of price with the punishment including a prison sentence for offenders. In the absence of this, the market will continue to be ruled by the unscruplous element to make a fast buck would lack protection[4].

Investment on Corporate Securities

Though there are several investment avenues left open for the investing public for making investment, as pointed out in the scope of the study in the first chapter of the present stock, the study examines only the grievance, the investors connected with corporate investment and legal aspects/framework connected with investors' protection for such investments. Fig. 2.2 portrays the need for investors' protection.

Figure 2.2

Need for Investors' Protection

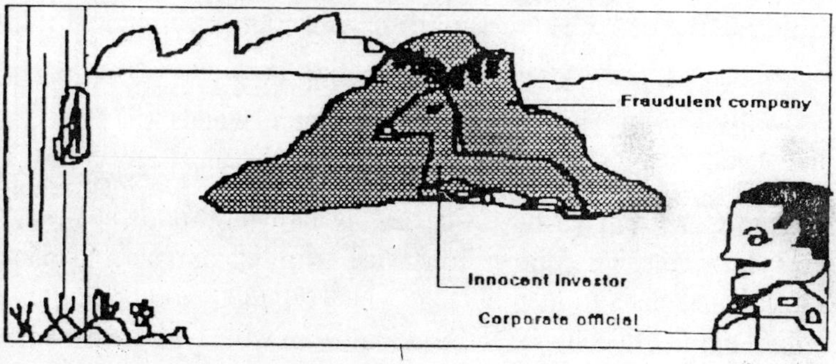

Legislative Protection to Investors

The table given below shows the nature of complaints and the remedies available to the investor under law. Aggrieved investors can lodge their complaints in writing with the companies, regional stock exchanges, Registrar of Companies, Company Law Board, Debenture Trustees and SEBI. The investors can also have an action against the erring companies through consumer forums.

The Companies Act and the Listing Agreement of the Stock Exchange provide certain safeguards for the investors. The normal complaints against companies and the protection available are listed below:

TABLE I

Nature of Complaints Against Companies Under Various Legislations and Relife Provided

Sl. No.	Complaints	Legislative Provision	Relief Provided
1.	Delay in refund of excess application money or allottment letters	Sec 73 of the Companies Act as amended in 1988	Payment of interest for the delayed period beyond 70 days from the closure of subscription list @ 15%
2.	Delay in transfer of shares	Sec 113 of the Companies Act	A time limit of two months provided in the Act for effecting transfer. As per the Listing Agreement, the time limit is only one month from the lodgement of shares
3.	Refusal of transfer shares	Section 22 (A) of SC (R) Act. This section lists the reasons for which transfer of shares can be refused	Transfer can be refused only for specific and valid reasons given in the Act and not otherwise
4.	Problem of odd lots	Listing Agreement provides for issue of certificates in marketable lots and avoidable of odd lots	Need for consolidation of odd lots and ensuring the issue of shares only in marketable lot through coversion of debentures or rights issue, provision of an odd lot trading session and listing out broker willing to trade

Contd....

TABLE I (Contd...)

Sl. No.	Complaints	Legislative Provision	Relief Provided
5.	Take-over bids	New clauses of 40 (a) and 40 (b) of listing agreement	Purchase or acquisition of shares beyond 5% to be notified to the stock exchange, Acquisition beyond 10% puts an obligation on the transfer and intermediary to notify the stock exchange and the public; and offer to the other share holders of the company to buy at offer price or the highest market price during the preceding six months
6.	Insider trading, rigging and other malpractices	SEBI (insider Trading) Regulations 1993	The investors have to guard themselves regarding the price and their investments, besides making complaint to SEBI
7.	Delay and non payments of interest/fixed deposits by companies	Section 58 (B) of the Companies Act	Appeal to the Company Law Board.
8.	Delay and non payments of dues or non-delivery of shares etc., by brokers	Rules and Bye-laws, of the stock exchange.	Complaint to the grievance cell of the stock exchange concerned.
9.	Non supply of debenture trust deed, refusal to inspection	Secs. 163, 196 219, 304 of the Companies Act.	Appeal to Company Law Board and lodge complaint with Trustee

Source : Sanjiv Agarwal, A Manual of Indian Capital Markets, p. 198.

Summary

As the individual investor community and the investment avenues are on the rise, it is interesting to know how the investors shall be protected through various legislations. The positive attitude of investors in investment of shares or securities was however, shaken by the share scandal in the year 1992. Eventhough there are various opportunities available for investment, investors are scared of investing in companies. In this situation, the investor protection becomes highly essential. The present chapter portrays a clear picture of the main features of the legislations meant for investor protection. The discussion on whether the legal enactments such as

1. SEBI Act, 1992
2. Securities Contract (Regulation) Act, 1956
3. Companies Act, 1956 are sufficient to protect the interest of investors or not?

follows the succeeding chapters of the present research report.

References

1. R.A. Stevenson, Fundamentals of Finance, McGraw International Book Inc. p. 12.
2. K. Sethuraman, "SEBI, Guidelines for Investor Protection Some Suggestions: The Economic Times, Bombay, June 23, 1992, p. 10.
3. The Economic Times, dated 23.03.92.
4. T. Bhanu, No Cover for Small Investors, Financial Express, 15.06.92.

3

Companies Act, 1956

Introduction

Soon after the Independence, the corporate sector in India underwent a sweeping change which could be understood in multiplication of joint stock companies and the investment in the paid up capital of public limited companies which was only Rs. 949 crores in 1961 rose to Rs. 2, 00,211 crores in December 1990[1]. The corporate enterprises have been the main instrument of economic development of almost every developed country outside the communist block. They have helped the economies of these countries to take a long leap forward by scientific management of their resources, both financial and non financial. The large scale operations have helped them to gain the dual advantage of optimization of return on the one hand and minimisation of costs on the other. It is evident that the form of business organisation has made inroads in to the distribution sector as well as service sector. Therefore, it would not be wrong if the level of growth of the of corporate sector is taken as a good measure of the level of growth economy as a whole.

Inspite of the extraordinary importance being attached to the growth of public sector through the state planning process, there has been an appreciable growth of private corporate sector in India. It has become the third largest shareholding population nation in the world with about 40 million shareholders which was only about one million a decade ago[2]. All these have made investors domestic population fascinated to commit their funds in the stock market. Therefore, investors' protection from Companies Act, 1956 is quite significant. The object of the company law is to provide for an effective protection to the investors, creditors and public at large. While at the same time, leaving management free to employ its energies competently in pursuit of company's objects.

Administration of Company Law

The Central Government has the overall responsibility for the administration of the Act. The administration is done through the Department of Company Affairs. The Central Government has been given various powers under the relevant Sections of the Act. According to Section 637, the Central Government can delegate these powers on one or more authorities established under the Act. But the powers to appoint public trustee under Section 153-A, and the power to make rules for the enforcement of the Companies Act under Section 642 cannot be delegated by it. Most of the powers it has already delegated to one or the other authority created under the Act. The authorities concerned with the administration of the Act are as follows:

1. Company Law Board : This is the principal agency for the administration of company law.
2. Registrar of Companies : The various company documents and returns are required to be filed with the Registrar.
3. Company Law Advisory Committee.

The Advisory Committee may consist of not more than five persons with suitable qualifications. As it is only an advisory body, neither the Central Government nor the Company Law Board is bound to accept its advice.

Investors require better protection when it comes to speculation and fluctuations in an overheated stock market. In this connection, it is worthwhile to mention the grievances faced by the investors.

Kinds of Grievances[3]

1. Non receipt of refund orders and allotment letters (60%-70% belong to this type).
2. Non receipt of dividend on shares, interest on debentures and interest on fixed deposits (about 6% of the complaints comprise these).
3. Non receipt of share and debenture certificates, complaints are approximately 18% of the total.
4. Non receipt of annual report, rights form, bonus shares, dividend, interest and interest on delayed receipt of refund order (these amount for another 16% of the complaints).

Other grievances faced by the investors

1. Investors are not getting dividend warrants and refund orders in time.
2. Sometimes dividends get delayed and then no amount of reminder-writing can squeeze a response. This can be seen while dealing in non specified shares.
3. Delay in refund of allotment money, receipt of dividend and share transfer.
4. Companies' dividend percentages are uncertain.

Therefore, caution should be the watch word. However if cheated, one must know investors' rights and procedures for obtaining justice. The important provisions of the Companies Act, 1956 connected with the investors' protection are listed below:

Legal Provisions Meant for Investors' Protection

Sec 59–deals with penalty for error in the issue of prospectus.

Sec 62-has to do with civil liabilities for misstatement in the prospectus.

Sec 63–spells out criminal liability for the misstatement in the prospectus.

Sec 68–deals with penalty for fraudulently inducing persons to invest. (In the above cases, Department of Company Affairs has to take action.)

Sec 73, 73 (2A), 73(2B)–interest on delayed refund and penalty against defaulting companies.

Sec 73 (1A), 73(2)–for listing of the securities of the company to be granted permission within 10 weeks of closing of subscription list.

Sec 58 (A), 58(4) (9), 58 (A) (10)–repayment of deposits in accordance with terms and conditions and right to approach Company Law Board.

Sec 84–issue of duplicate share certificates.

Sec 113, 113(2)–Company in normal circumstances delivers share/debenture certificates within 3 months of allotment with fine of Rs.500 for every day of of default.

Sec 111, 111 (2) 111(3), 111(4)–Company to register transfer and deliver share/debenture certificates within 3 months of allotment with fine of Rs. 500 for every day of default.

In this context, it is worth to examine the legal provisions of the Companies Act, 1956 meant for investors' protection and their effectiveness, inadequacies under the Companies Act, 1956.

Effectiveness of the Legal Provisions

There is a discussion on the effectiveness or otherwise to the provisions of the Indian Companies Act, 1956 connected with investors' protection in the following passages. The Sachar Committee's recommendations have been by and large taken into account in the Company Law Amendment Bill, but some significant ones have not been included and these are:–

★ The right to speak and the right to vote on show of hands to be extended to proxy holders. (This may give rise to professional proxies!).

★ The right to expel a member from a company, regardless

of provision in the Articles of Association, needs to be prohibited.

★ Activities of brokers mobilising deposits to be regulated.

The following recommendations and suggestions from the professional bodies and chambers were not likewise incorporated in the Bill:

★ Compulsory insurance cover for deposits up to Rs. 10,000.

★ Fixing time limit for paying interim dividend.

★ Remitting consolidated and uniform stamp duty on securities to facilitate prompt issue.

★ Harmonisation of statutory provisions meant for investors' protection under one legislation and one authority.

Analysis

It is observed that the companies which come out with public issues are expected to keep the share application monies received in a separate bank account in any scheduled bank, as per sub-section 3 of section 73 of the Companies Act, 1956. The object of this sub-section was to serve as a protection to the investor's money.

Though the Companies Act, 1956 does not define the term 'allotment' it was explained by judiciary thus 'what is termed allotment' is generally neither more or less than the acceptance by the company of the offer to take shares. To take the common case, the offer is to take a certain number of shares or such a less number of shares as may be allotted. That offer is accepted by the allotment either of the total number mentioned in the offer or a less number, to be taken by the person who made the offer.

Thus it is clear that till the allotment is made and the listing in a stock exchange is completed, the issuing company has no right to the share application monies and these monies at that stage do not form part of the assets of the company. The relationship between the applicants on the one hand and the company is that of a bailor and bailee at this stage and not that of creditor and a debtor. The point is, if the company fails to obtain minimum subscription or fails to allot the shares of fails to get its share listed in a recognised stock exchange at that stage, it was bound to refund the monies so received to the applicants. It is also observed that the companies which were going public could access the funds mobilised, only after a time gap which could cover a minimum period of ten weeks before which it cannot complete all the formalities. Though, till early eighties, this delay did not mean much, the eighties saw several established companies tapping the share market and the cost conscious promoters eyed the idle funds in the share application monies account. Since the object of a separate account for this purpose was explained as an effective trust created by the statute to protect the interests of the investors, the possibilities of amendments to the Companies Act, 1956 was a distant vision.

It was during this period, the concept of 'Bridge Finance' came into existence. Any short term advance which is to be repaid from an identifiable and certain source of funds could be referred to as a 'bridge'. Actually, what is being bridged is the time gap rather than the gap in finance. The 'bridge' effectively closed the time gap for a company that came up in paying up its commitments and the receipt of funds. These companies had to meet the project costs which they were incurring even as the issue was on and could have access to the funds so mobilised only after a time gap.

Bridge finance initially took the shape of meeting the requirements of a company before a state subsidy could be obtained. It was not originally thought of, as a source to meet the capital requirements before the completion of share issue. In eighties, however, financial institutions came up with specific schemes of offering bridging loans against public issue of share capital.

Bridge loans can also be granted against public issue of shares upto 90 per cent of the underwriting commitment of the institutions. To be eligible to draw the amount of bridging loan against public issue of shares, the promoters should have brought in their contribution in full (either as share capital or as interest free unsecured loan) and the assisted concern should itself have availed of loan assistance to the extent of 90 per cent sanctioned to it.

The security for such bridge loan against public issue of shares is the joint and several guarantee of the promoters and pledge, wherever feasible, of fully paid-up shares to the extent of at least 51 per cent of the paid up capital under their direct control. The bridge loans granted against public issue of shares are to be repaid out of the proceeds of the public issue and a suitable provision to this effect is made in the prospectus issued for raising the requisite capital.

It is to be noted that the investors' friendly provision sought to be included in the Companies Act, was negated by the introduction of a scheme which blantantly built in all the measures to circumvent it. If the object of the bridge loan was to accelerate the project momentum, the emphasis should have been on the assets that were to be created out of this bridge loan and which should have served as its primary security. But by linking up the bridge loan directly to the public issue and by claiming the paid-up value of such shares to be the security cover, the scheme opened out an opportunity for the unscrupulous to take advantage of.

The auditors of the banks also classified these loans 'secured' when the only security available in many cases were the shares, this bridge finance helped the promoters to subscribe to.

Spate of Public Issue

Come nineties, one saw a spate of public issue and the bridge loans went to shore up share prices in the market rather than to any constructive usage-creation of assets and such other–which could provide at least a security cover if needed. The other day a stock broker who did not want to be identified spoke of the build-up that is made over a couple of years to take the shares to the peak. He lamented that this two year period is sought to be compressed to less than six months these days!

The method which was used during the phase was undoubtedly usage of bridge finance. Thus, a financing method advocated to accelerate project implementation was sought to be used to boost share prices in the market. Thus, the misuse is due to the players in the market, but it is also true that the misuse was made possible by the wrong structuring of finance. That the scheme itself was designed in such a way that a statutory protection given to the hapless investor was done away with, has been overlooked for so long.

Misuse of funds

These are the views of the opponents of the scheme of bridge finance against public issue of share capital. Their grouse is that Reserve Bank of India (RBI) had slept on this matter too long and even RBI's recent move banning further grant of bridge loan is being seen by them as a measure to close the stables which are already empty.

On the other hand, the supporters of this scheme of financing argue that the scheme had worked very well along and the misuse is of recent origin. While all steps to prevent misuse should be welcome, withdrawing of the scheme altogether is not a step in the right direction.

Bridge finance against a fully underwritten issue does not violate any law whatsoever and there has been no public outcry against the scheme till recently. Many a first generation entrepreneur who have nothing to fall back upon and who are prevented from accessing the subscription monies till such allotment and listing are complete, keep the wheels of the project moving essentially with the assistance of the bridge finance and an overnight withdrawal has benumbed many of them.

While the scheme was alright, the structuring of it should have been such as to relate the financing to the creation of assets and towards financing their project cost and an effective check on the end use would have been more appropriate measure than to have linked the financing to the share issue aspect alone.

As in many others there is truth in both the arguments. The effect of the sudden withdrawal of bridge finance has affected many a project as well. There are indications that RBI is having second thoughts on the ban imposed on the granting such bridge finance. Perhaps it would like to build in several safety clauses and regulatory conditions or perhaps bridging finance against public issue of share capital may become a thing of the past one does not know. To bridge or not to bridge seems to be the main worry on the credit policy front these days.

Lapses in the Companies Act

Investors want a regulatory system which ensures transparency, fairness, and reduced transaction costs. As the regulatory functions are now split between the Securities and Exchange Board of India and the Department of Company Affairs, both should coordinate their functions. There seems to be a case for vesting the full responsibility on one of these two regulatory authorities. At present, a company issuing a prospectus has to get it cleared by both. Whichever agency is made responsible, the prime consideration should be the protection of the interest of investing public.

It will be remembered that the Companies Bill introduced in Parliament in 1993 was withdrawn in view for its many short comings, especially as it was not in tune with the new economic policy. It is expected that a revised bill will be introduced soon to protect the investors. It is therefore timely to bring to the attention of the Department of Company Affairs and the public too of the several urgently needed changes relating to prospectus and merges with the hope that they will be incorporated in the new Bill. In view of the urgency of the problems and the long time it will take to get a Comprehensive Companies Act passed through the Parliament, the Government should consider amending the existing Companies Act immediately. There are well established precedents for amending the existing law to implement urgently needed reforms, and then a bring forward a comprehensive amended Bill. The main inadequacy of the Companies Act is, the prospectus has not been reviewed. This has been clearly explained in the subsequent paragraphs.

(i) Reliable, Readable and Abridged Prospectus

Abridged prospectus gives rise to several difficulties. In order to reduce issue cost, Department of Company Affairs has, by a notification dated October 3, 1991, permitted companies to issue an abridged version of the prospectus. The notification has also prescribed the contents of such abridged version. It is required to contain the salient features of the complete prospectus. The Companies Act prescribes various civil liabilities and punishments for misstatements in a prospectus. In case of misstatements, an applicant for shares or other securities can even seek to avoid the contract to take up the shares and ask for his money back. For the removal of all doubts, it may be spelt out that these rules and remedies apply equally to the abridged version also. The SEBI requires the lead manager/merchant banker certificate deals only with the complete prospectus and not the abridged version. This needs to be corrected.

There are three main difficulties of the abridged version:

1. It is generally printed in such small type that it is virtually unreadable except by the most persevering persons. Can one expect the promoters to print the abridged version so as to be easily readable, without straining the eyes?
2. It is observed that, in practice one finds that the abridged version is printed on a single sheet along with the application form. The reverse side of the application form, which is submitted to the company through the bankers for collection along with the application money contains important details. Therefore, an applicant has either to make a copy or obtain another blank form if he wants to retain for his records and future reference a copy of the representation made by the directors, on the faith of which he has applied for the securities. The objective of cost reduction gets lost in this process. It will help if only one application form is printed along a perforated line, in each abridged prospectus as contemplated in the circular dated January 9, 1992, enabling the applicant to retain the representation made by the Directors.
3. As the full prospectus is not available to the public freely,

it is not possible to check whether the abridged version contains all the salient features of the complete prospectus. Most likely, it does, because the SEBI has to approve the abridged version as well as the full prospects. However, there has been instance of abridged prospectus referring the reader of the full prospectus, on certain key matters. The lead manager/merchant banker may be required to include in his 'due diligence' certificate a paragraph to the effect that the abridged version fairly sets out all the salient features of the complete prospectus. This is particularly relevant in respect of the assumption underlying the profit projections, the justification for the premium, if any, and the risk factors. The contents of the prospectus and its abridged versions, as per the company law notifications, do not specially call for the disclosure of the basis of pricing the securities, and the justification for the premium, if any.

The SEBI has adopted the position that the market should determine the pricing and has not prescribed any formula. It has left it to the issuing company to fix the premium, if any, but requires the net assets value of the company and the justification for the premium to the disclosed (by existing companies). However, in respect of issues of non-residents, the Ministry of Industry has laid down some guidelines (press note dated June 8, 1994) inter alia, with the objective of making "both investment and disinvestment market related' Accordingly, the Government has decided to apply the following guidelines:

Every preferential allotment of shares by companies (allotment of shares other than allotment on rights basis) shall be at market value of the shares. The issue price shall be determined on the basis of their average price during the immediate preceding six months at the main listing centre. This would be calculated on the monthly average of the high and low rates quoted for the shares at such centres. Is there any reason why the spirit underlying these guidelines (making the prices market related) should not apply to domestic issues also (whether or not on preferential terms)?

To ask for the full prospectus to be made available freely will go counter, to the objective of reducing the costs of issue securities in the primary market. At the same time, it is necessary, in the interests of transparency and fairness, to the pricing basis and the justification for the premium known to the public. Therefore, SEBI has required that these should be disclosed in the abridged prospectus also, while approving it. Some abridged versions provide justification for the premium, citing qualitative and quantitative factors. A reference is made to projected earnings per share and a case is made out, citing industry studies appearing in various periodicals, that the Price/Earnings multiple used is a conservative one, and therefore the premium is reasonable.

(ii) Attempting to violate the provisions of the Companies Act, 1956 with regard to the issue of duplicate share certificates has occured recently in the country. The recent episode in India namely, the issue of duplicate shares by Ms Rajul Vasa and members of her family by Reliance Consultancy Services (RCS) is a pertinent point to be mentioned here. A discussion on the cases illustrating the violation of the provisions of Companies Act, 1956 is given in the following passages[4]:–

Issue of Duplicate Share Certificates by Reliance Consultancy Services

The controversy relating to Ms Rajul Vasa and members of the family in respect of duplicate share issues and switching of Reliance Industries Ltd. (RIL) by its registrars, Reliance Consultancy Services (RCS) and others raised several questions about the extent of such shares likely to be in circulation, the possible misuse of the systems by RIL and its satellite companies to gain undue financial advantages, the role of the registrar–a company with close organic links with RIL and so forth. In this context, it is worthwhile to mention here, the breakup units of shares in duplicate issue by the RCS to Ms Rajul Vasa and her family. This is presented in the following table:

TABLE II

Details of the Issue of Duplicate Shares by RCS

Date of the Issue	Number of Duplicate Shares Issued
14.07.94	10,950
22.08.94	28,203
11.09.94	726
Total	**39,879**

Source: Interim Report of SEBI, Bombay.

Lapses in the Companies Act, 1956

It has been observed that, there are lapses in the Companies Act, 1956 in different situations and they are given below:

1. In the case of issue of duplicate shares to Ms Rajul Vasa and her family, the procedural aspects reveal the following lapses:
   (i) Original letters or applications requesting for the issue of duplicate share certificates have not been maintained by the company, and hence they were not produced for verification.
   (ii) The indemnity bonds were not executed and stamped.
2. In another case, RCS issued 3,774 duplicate share certificates to Mangla Investment Ltd. under various ledger folios of the company, the indemnity bond was given on a plain paper.
3. In another case, Reliance Consultancy Services (RCS) has sent split up shares to R T Sha, which were returned undelivered by the postal authorities and were subsequently lost or misplaced in the office of RCS, and duplicate shares were issued without obtaining indemnity bond.

4. In another case, Oriental Insurance Corporation (OIC) has applied for 29,400 rights shares on December 7, 1987, when it was found that OIC has not received the said shares, it informed RCS about the loss of these shares on June 15, 1993. When RCS communicated to OIC the procedure for issue of duplicate shares, OIC requested RCS to waive the condition of public notice keeping in view the fact that OIC is a public sector company.

RCS agreed to waive the condition regarding public notice. OIC submitted indemnity bond in August 1994. The duplicate share certificates were issued on November 21, 1994.

The inspection teams from SEBI recommended that some duplicate share certificates had been issued while the original certificates in existence, which fact was very much in the knowledge of RCS.

Considering the above, it is hoped that the Companies Bill to be introduced in the winter session of the parliament in 1995 will deal with prospectus and their abridged versions adequately public interest being given paramount consideration, and in the mean time necessary amendments be made in the existing Companies Act, 1956, especially in the issue of duplicate share certificates. But unfortunately the Companies Amendment Bill, 1995 was not introduced, and therefore did not come up for discussion and consideration in the winter session of Indian Parliament in December, 1995.

References

1. Statistical Outline of India, Tata Services Limited, Department of Economics and Statistics, 1991-92.
2. M R Mayya, Securities Market: Part I–Recent Trends, The Economic Times, Bangalore, 17th Jan. 1990, p.5.
3. G.V. Ramakrishna, "Investors' Protection", Business World, Nov. 1994, p. 12.
4. SEBI report on RIL Switch, Dulpication, the Economic Times, February 7, 1996, Edition, p. 22.

4

Securities Contracts (Regulation) Act, 1956

The main drawbacks of Indian capital market prior to the enactment of Securities Contracts (Regulations) Act were as follows:

(i) Lack of uniformity and control

(ii) No restriction on membership

(iii) No check on unhealthy speculation

(iv) No regulations on listing of securities.

Logically, there were share market crises and crashes ensured. This led to the appointment of certain committees to recommend suitable, measures for regulating the trading in stock and shares. A draft Bill, prepared in 1951, referred to an expert committee under the Chairmanship of Shri. A.D. Gorwala, became the Securities Contracts (Regulation) Act, 1956.

Effectiveness of SCRA

The Securities Contracts (Regulation) Act 1956, (SCRA) was enacted to provide for the regulation of stock exchanges and of transactions in securities dealt on them with a view to preventing undesirable speculations in them. The scheme of the regulation contemplated by the Act provides for–

(i) Recognition of stock exchanges

(ii) General control over brokers trading methods and practices

(iii) Regulations of contracts and options in securities and

(iv) Provision relating to listing of securities by public companies.

Recognition

According to the Securities Contracts (Regulation) Act, 1956 every stock exchange should get recognition from the Central Government and any amendments or modifications must be similarly approved. Government for functioning and a recognized stock exchange, thus is a powerful guardian of the interests of the general public.

Any stock exchange which desirous of being recognized may make an application in the prescribed manner to the Central Government with all the prescribed particulars. The Central Government may grant recognition to the stock exchange if it is satisfied, after making necessary enquiries and obtaining such further information, if any, as it may require:

(a) that the rules and bye-laws of stock exchanges are in conformity with such conditions as may be prescribed in order to ensure fair dealing and to protect investors;

(b) that the stock exchange is willing to comply with any other conditions (including condition as to the number of members) which the Central Government, in consultation with the governing body of the stock exchange and having regard to (1) the area served by the stock exchange; (2) the standing; and (3) the nature of securities dealt with in it, may impose for the purpose of carrying out the objects of Securities Contracts (Regulation) Act, 1956 and

(c) that it would be in the interest of trade and also in the public interest.

The rules of a recognized stock exchange, the powers of management of its governing body and its constitution (including the appointment thereon of not more than three Government nominees), the admission of members, the qualifications for membership, the exclusion, suspension and readmission of members, the registration of partnership and the appointment of authorized representatives and clerks must be duly approved by Government. These rules can be amended, varied or rescinded only with the precious approval of Government. Likewise, the bye-laws of the recognized exchange providing in detail for the regulation and control of contracts in securities and for every aspect of the trading activities of members must also be sanctioned by government and any amendments or modifications must be similarly approved. Government's authority extends much further to make or demand suomoto any rules or bye-laws of a recognized stock exchanges, if it so considers desirable in the interest of trade and in public interest.

The Act empowered the Government with even more drastic powers – the power to make enquiries into the affair of recognized stock exchange and its business, and lastly, to withdraw the recognition granted to an exchange should such steps be deemed indispensable in the interest of trade and in public interest. Government has thus complete control over the recognized stock exchange.

The recognition shall be granted if the Central Government has satisfied about the particulars either on permanent basis or for such period not less than one year as may be prescribed in the recognition. Bombay, Calcutta, Delhi, Madras, Ahmedabad, Hyderabad, Bangalore and Indore have so far granted permanent recognition and other stock exchanges are granted temporary recognition for a period of a 5 years at a time. Every grant of recognition of stock exchange shall be published in the Gazette of India and also in the Official Gazette of the State in which the principal office of the stock exchange is situated, and such recognition shall have effect as from the date of its publication in the Gazette of India . Every recognized stock exchange shall furnish to the Central Government a copy of the annual report, and such annual report shall contain such particulars as may be prescribed. The Central Government shall refuse the recognition only after giving an opportunity to the stock exchange concerned to be heard in the matter, and the reasons for such refusal shall be communicated to the stock exchange in writing. The Central

Government imposes the restrictions towards recognition due to protection of investors.

Present Recognised Stock Exchanges

At present, there are 23 stock exchanges recognized under the Securities Contracts (Regulation) Act, 1956. A stock exchange has also been set up at Gangtok, in Sikkim State early in 1986. No. recognition has been sought for this body as the jurisdiction of the Securities Contracts (Recognition) Act, 1956 has not so far been extended to the areas covered by the State. The various stock exchanges, and their addresses are given in the Appendix I of the present research report.

Regulations on Trading

As regards the regulations on trading in the ring of the exchange, the stock exchange authorities operate a variety of regulations in the following ways to protect the interests of investors:

1. Only authorised clerks of the members are permitted to enter the trading ring with their badges. Souda Block Books are provided by the stock exchange. Entry into the trading ring restricted to members and their authorised clerks. The inspectors of the stock exchange visit the ring and check the presence of unauthorised persons, any indiscipline or voilence or other acts. Persons involved in such acts could be removed from the trading ring, suspended or punished otherwise. The security guards provide physical help to inspectors.
2. The Monitoring Department of the exchange keeps a watch on the price movements and trading volume of the members and take such action as is necessary to control excessive trading and speculative fervour. It may impose adhoc margins, suspend trading and enquire into any special developments.
3. In the case of any disputes on the trading floor, the floor committee can officially intervene and give their judgement and in the case of settlement objections, an admin-

istrative committee will go into the matter.

4. In any other disputes, the lower bench, the full bench or the Governing Board may examine and give their decisions and certain matters of dispute are referred to a special committee appointed by the Executive Director.
5. The Operations Department of the stock exchange will supervise the operations, make any announcements at the time of trading, suspension of trading or collections of quotations, giving of company information, and so forth. The fixation of different types of margins, making of prices, supervision of trading and the like are the responsibility of the Executive Director. The auctions of shares and related matters connected with settlement are looked into by the Operations Department.

Option Trading

Indian stock markets are undergoing material changes in their functioning for the last few years. The Indian Government has realised, after 40 years of policies of protectionism, that no economy can live in isolation. One should think the same is true about stock markets. Stock markets are places where the investors have chances for buying and selling shares for money. Also, the operators and traders have chances of converting their imagination of the future prices of the share into business deals and as such the stock market provides room for speculation. The four metropolitan stock exchanges have trading in specific, that is, modified "modified badla" as well as cash list.

The limitation of the modified badla system in terms of transparency, foreplay and the not so sufficient tools of risk management had been realised over the years. However, in the absence of proper tools like futures and options, the modified badla system was providing the much needed liquidity to the market place. The modified badla system is the creation of business prudency of Indian capital markets and is unique to India. The exchanges having cash list only, like Vadodara stock exchange (VSE), cannot however, deny the presence of ramphant speculation in certain scripts. One has the person interested as investors only and operators interested as traders only operating on the same level ground whereas, the requirements of the two and the requirements of the authorities for the two are totally different. One at VSE strongly believes that for the efficiency and fair play of the marketplace, speculation needs to be taken out of the cash list. Speculation is not a dirty thing but it needs to leave absolutely different ground rules. This can ensure rolling settlements in the cash list and avoid frequent failures, clubbing of settlements and other problems of investors.

Economic Significance of Options

Options provide investors with the opportunity to hedge investments in the underlying shares and share portfolios and can thus significantly reduce the overall risk related to the investments.

In addition, options and futures contracts increase liquidity and reduce price fluctuations in the underlying shares. As a result, the risk level associated with investment in a company's shares will normally make it easier and cheaper to raise new risk capital.

A well-organised options market thus makes an important contribution to the fulfilment by the stock exchange of one of its most important objectives, namely, to establish the best possible conditions for quoted companies to raise capital at a low cost. The respondents views on this system have been examined in chapter VII of the present research report.

Listing Regulations

Listing means admission of shares of a company to trading on the stock exchange and to a quotation of its share price. It is not obligatory by statute for a company to enlist shares on the stock exchanges. However, if a company declares its intention in the prospectus to enlist its shares on a stock exchange, it is obligatory to do so. A public limited company making a public issue through prospectus or borrows from all-India financial institutions or banks make a condition on a company or the

Government as matter of policy in the public interest can compel a company to enlist its shares in the stock exchange (sec.21 of SC (R) Act, 1956) the company has to get its shares listed on stock exchange, thereby to safeguard the interest of the investors.

Eligibility for Listing

Any company is eligible for listing if

1. The company is a public limited company;
2. The minimum paid-up capital is Rs. 3 crores; and
3. It is offering to the public for subscription through prospectus atleast 60% of its paid-up capital;

The listed companies are expected to have a standard denomination of shares of Rs. 100 and Rs. 10 and that minimum lots of allotment should in multiples of that face value. The requirements of minimum public offer of 60% is flexible and modified according to the Government policy and depends on the capital structure of the company and nature of activities of industries to which it belongs.

Regulations for Listed Companies

1. A listed company in contrast to a new company is forced to make an application to the exchange in the prescribed form for listing its new securities.
2. For listing bonus shares, rights shares/debentures, the company should apply in the prescribed form.
3. A company having a paid-up capital of more than Rs. 5 crores has to get its shares listed on one or more stock exchange besides the nearest stock exchange.
4. After the prospectus is advertised and applications received, the allotment of shares has to be made within the time limits, as permitted by the SEBI and in the manner agreed to by the exchange. In the allotment, the lower category of applicants, namely, those of 500 shares, will have to be given greater weightage than those in the higher categories.

5. Subscription list should be kept open for a minimum of two and a maximum of 10 working days if the issue is underwritten by public financial institutions, and up to 21 days if the issue is not so underwritten.
6. The company should complete the allotment process within the time limit of 10 weeks from the date of closure of the subscription list and it has to pay 15% interest in respect of excess application money for the delayed period beyond 10 weeks.
7. There are also provisions governing the retention of oversubscription, time limit for allotment of shares and refusal orders and distribution of share certificates after the final allotment respectively.
8. Application moneys have to be refunded if the subscription amount falls short of 90% of the total amount offered to public.

Benefits of Listing of Securities

Following are the benefits and protection provided by stock exchanges in listing of securities to the investors:-

(a) The regular and latest reports on listed companies, help the investors in saving for investments in the securities of the company which are listed on stock exchange.

(b) The companies are under an obligation in terms of listing agreement to inform its investors about the various corporate information, and therefore the listed companies constantly approaching unintentionally to the investor from time to time.

(c) The transaction in listed securities are published widely in the leading periodicals and journals and therefore corporate details like the results, dividend announcements, expansion and diversification plan of the listed companies are published from time to time.

(d) On account of liquidity, marketability and free transferability which are conferred by the listing of securities on a stock exchange, securities of the listed company qualify for preferential treatment for investment by institutional investors and foreign investors.

(e) An official quotation on the floor of the stock exchange is an important indicator to the company as well as to the investors as prices are arrived at publicly on the basis of demand and supply .

(f) Listing of shares results in improved marketability as the confidence of investor is enhanced due to regulation of stock exchanges trading procedures, greater liquidity, reduced risk and so forth. These in turn influence price of a share.

(g) Listed companies also enjoy certain concessions under the direct tax laws and official quotations are accepted by tax authorities. If the shares are quoted on a stock exchange, the company will be treated as a company in which public are substantially interested.

(h) Listing requirements provide for compulsory and timely disclosures of corporate information relating to bonus (or) rights issue, advance notice for closing the Register of Members, facilities for transfer, registration of rights and fair and equitable allotment in securities.

5

SEBI Act, 1992

Several taken by the Government of India during nineties will lead to gradual globalisation of the Indian capital market, with the securities of Indian companies being held by investors worldwide and traded on global stock exchanges. Given the changing economic scenario, Indian capital market will present enormous opportunities to the private and public sector companies to tap their requirements of resources.

Emergence of SEBI

The decade of 1980s witnessed a phenomenal growth and development of the securities markets in India. For the first time, the Indian securities market demonstrated its potential not only to mobilise the savings of the household sector but also to allocate it with some degree of efficiency for industrial development. By the end of the decade, the securities market in India came to be firmly integrated with the financial system of the country. With the corporate sector increasingly relying on the securities market for meeting their long-term requirement of funds, the securities market competed on equal terms with the development financial institutions which were the traditional purveyors of longterm capital. This brought about notable changes in the capital structure of the companies across industries, gave birth to new intermediaries and institutions in the securities market and created a new awareness and interest in investment opportunities in the securities market among investors. Inspite of these developments and the quantitative expansion of the market, its quality lagged far behind, and there was absence of adequate professionalism and fair competition among the various players in the market. Besides, the regulatory framework then prevailing was fragmented, which made regulatory supervision and its enforcement difficult, if not ineffective.

Market development is predicted on a sound, fair and transparent regulatory framework. To sustain the growth of the market and crystallise the growing pool of investors, it was essential to remove the trading malpractices and structural inadequacies prevailing in the market, and provide the investors an organised, well regulated market place in whose probity they can have confidence, where their rights are fully protected and redressal made easily accessible and effective. The Government therefore, felt the need for setting up of an apex body for the first time, exclusively for investor protection and for the protection of orderly and healthy growth of the securities market. Accordingly, the Securities and Exchange Board of India was constituted on April 12, 1988 through an Administrative Resolution as an intrim body under the overall administrative control of the Ministry of Finance, as a precursor to the Statutory Board. After the promulagation of the Securities and Exchange Board of India ordinance on January 30, 1992, SEBI was established as a statutory body on February 21, 1992. Subsequently, the ordinance was replaced by the Securities and Exchange Board of India Act on April 4, 1992.

SEBI Achievements

1. SEBI has become and begun as an agency policing the different market players in the capital market bringing about a qualitative improvement in the functioning of these various players, though it had to face a lot of flak and lack of cooperation from them. However, SEBI has been able to bring round the stock exchanges, the stock brokers, the mutual funds, the lead managers, the Registrars to accept a code of conduct and transparency and openness in their dealings.

2. The control on capital issues has been abolished and free pricing of securities has been introduced in keeping with the flavour of liberalisation measures. As a result, today the public issue of other securities can be priced according to the judgement of the corporate managements provided the norms set by SEBI are followed.
3. SEBI has made the stock exchanges accept broad basing of membership of these stock exchanges so that a larger body of investors are enabled to avail to buy-and-sell facilities for shares and other securities. The closed-club character of the stock exchange is therefore gradually changing for the better.
4. The governing boards of stock exchanges have been made more representative of non-broker element and thus decisions to suit the vested interests of the brokers in their own have been made more difficult. Justice for the investor is made more easily obtainable from stock exchanges. Almost all stock exchanges will in future have representatives of Government, SEBI, public and the investor community and thus accountable to SEBI and not play to the tune "His Master's Voice".
5. New members of the stock exchanges will be drawn from different allied professions like chartered accountants, company secretaries and MBAs. Resultantly innovation and professional approach will be available and can be expected from the stock brokers. A gradual qualitative operational improvement could therefore be expected accordingly.
6. Institutional corporate membership is encouraged by SEBI and soon bank's subsidiaries, finance companies and broker firms with huge resources will become members of stock exchange in future. Commanding huge resources, availing professional talent and subject to more discipline like audit and inspection, these corporate members will be able to cater to a large clientele throughout the country and also open branch offices at more centres and

thus provide cheap, convenient and efficient service to investors, thanks to SEBI.

7. At present, even members with very little resources can do business without any limit and therefore bring the investors into great risk in case of default or financial crunch or for similar reasons. To meet this contingency, SEBI has imposed capital adequacy norms for regulating the business of brokers to avoid over-trading. Eight per cent of the total turnover has to be maintained as capital at all times and thus brokers cannot overreach turnovers putting the investors to business risks.
8. SEBI has also imposed a condition that contracts issued by brokers should mention the purchase or sale price separately and commission charged should be separately to enable investors to have full information of the deals.
9. All market players including merchant bankers, stock exchanges, mutual funds, brokers, sub-brokers, foreign institutional investors, underwriters, advisors to public issues and Registrars have to be registered with SEBI and cannot operate without a licence from SEBI. SEBI will have the right of inspection of the books, registers and other documents of these players and will also have the right to hear, deal with and punish them for their lapses and thus bring about better and improved methods of investor service.
10. As refunds of application monies have caused inconvenience of investors and in order to make the float money arising out of public issues subscriptions, a new instrument of stock invest has been introduced. Though stock invest, applicants do not have to wail for refunds and their own monies will earn interest in these accounts. Though there are some problems in the use of stock invest, it has greatly helped the investors to have some relief available through this instrument.
11. SEBI has also arranged for its own nominee at the time of finalisation of allotment for public issues being present to ensure that there are no malpractices in allotment.

SEBI has also proposals for appointment of actual investors on the governing board of stock exchanges for looking after the interests of investors[1].

12. SEBI has been given prosecution powers to take necessary action against issuing companies directly. This power is intended to provide speedy justice to the investing community.

13. SEBI has been empowered to impose penalty not exceeding Rs. 10,000 for failure to redress investors' grievances by an intermediary.

Inadequacies in SEBI's Function

SEBI has received 3.25 lac complaints from the investing community during the year 1992, and only a part of them could be resolved satisfactorily. SEBI needs teeth to take action against errant managements so that complaints of investors can be dealt with promptly and satisfactorily. Gradually, investors are getting disenchanted with SEBI, and it is therefore necessary for SEBI to take immediate steps to correct this situation.

SEBI's desicion of minimum subscription of shares from 100 to as much as 500 shares is a death blow for small investors. Inspite of protests and objections from investors' forums, SEBI has done this and in one stroke SEBI has distanced itself from the investors who may choose the mutual fund route only is wrong, illogical and unwarranted. Equity investment being a rich investment, it should be left to the choice of investors–mutual fund route or direct investment route.

SEBI has also found fault with for frequent issue of guidelines with no finality. SEBI not regulating the public issues hitting the market has resulted in bunching of issues affecting the capital market–sometimes even good issues failing. Some remedial steps are considered necessary. SEBI has not paid attention to take action against unauthorised share trading houses coming up throughout the country. These illegal trading houses' operations and their exploitations of investors requir~ ~o be looked into and regulated.

The recent episode, namely, M.S. Shoes case is a pertinent point where SEBI lost its credibility on account of inefficiency on the part of SEBI's officials. The facts of the M.S. Shoes case has been illustrated below.

Two charges that have been levelled against M.S. Shoes company were

1. Misleading investors by giving false information.
2. Promoters of that company have been given allotment which are against the SEBI's guidelines.

Officials of State Bank of India (SBI) capital markets have been accused for not checking the required documents, which were found to be inconsistent with SEBI's guidelines.

1. One of the guidelines which has been stipulated by SEBI is that the time gap between rights and public issues could not be more than 30 days was violated and time gap between two issues was relaxed.
2. Advertisement depicted cum right price instead of ex-right price.

SEBI also should try to establish a cadre of top executives for manning higher level posts in the stock exchanges. There is a dearth of trained, experienced and suitable personnel for the post of executive directors and SEBI has to attend to this matter urgently.

Remedial Measure for Investor' Protection

[2]The fundamental problems with India's primary market is the weakness of the market system and the legal system, as well as the enforcement machinery. Until these are strengthened, the investors are not grappling with the real problem. While the various guidelines issued by the Securities and Exchange Board of India (SEBI) do address these problems, they are not by themselves, strong enough to constitute a cure. What is required is a systematic solution rather than a legislative–control system, which is what most SEBI's guidelines provide for.

The current system seems to be control-oriented and works

through rules and regulations. However, in the absence of an effective law-enforcement machinery, they will continue to be broken. In fact, SEBI's guidelines are silent about the repercussions on market intermediaries when they break the rules. Moreover, SEBI is not strictly speaking, a law enforcement agency which puts it at the mercy of the country's sluggish legal system. By contrast, a systematic solution would discourage violators not only by making it difficult to engage in such transgressions of the law, but also by ensuring that they are fruitless. As part of such a solution, three specific measures could be taken to protect investors.

(a) Rating market intermediaries

(b) Introduction of bought out issues

(c) Scribbless trading.

Rating Market Intermediaries

Eliciting more professional services from market intermediaries will provide more investor protection, SEBI must institute a rating system for merchant bankers, underwriters, registrars, and project appraising institutions. And it should be mandatory for the intermediaries to declare their ratings in the prospectus and advertisements for the primary market issues, they are involved with the yardsticks for such ratings. The extent to which the intermediaries redress investors' grievances, disclosure information fairly, observe time schedule and adopt fair trade practices in their capital market operations.

Since the country has already credit industry, this exercise would simply mean an additional step for it. However, all the credit rating agencies in the country, the Credit Rating Information Services of India Limited (CRISIL), the Investment Information and Credit Rating Agency of India Ltd., and the Credit Analysis and Research Ltd., are are promoted by financial institutions, giving them a governmental flavour. This can be changed only if the private sector begins to play a bigger role in this industry.

Bought out Issues

Today, companies approach the public directly with their issues, which are managed by merchant bankers, or a consortium of merchant bankers, to buy out the entire issue from a company and sell it to the public. This would place on us on the merchant banker to set the price for an outright purchase of the issue.

It would also force him to peg it at a level that is neither too low for the company nor too high for the public to reject the issue. And, since the merchant bankers' credibility would be at stake, it would lead to greater professionalism in the field. Freed from the burden of raising public funds, companies would then be able to concentrate on their projects. Interestingly, such a system has already been brought into play at the Over The Counter Exchange of India (OTCEI).

Scribbless Trading

This would immediately eliminate problems relating to the despatch, transfer and registration of share certificates, right issues, bonus issues and Registrar's records by replacing the physical transfer of share certificates with accounting entries. Indeed, the country is gradually moving towards scripless trading. The National Stock Exchange started trading in equity operations on a limited scale, from Nov. 3rd, 1994 while the Bombay Stock Exchange has started electronic trading in the year 1995.

It is high time that SEBI lays on its weight behind such systematic solutions to the problems of the primary market, rather than adopting regulations which are fast becoming obselete. It has been observed that such a nationwide trading is implemented in India, then it provides greater liquidity and ease of transactions to the investors across the country.

Summary

The rampant malpractices noticed in the capital market stood in the way of infusing confidence to the investors which is necessary for mobilisation of larger quantity of funds from the public and promote the growth of the markets. Under these circumstances, there arose a need to constitute a larger body which can act as a unifying force in bringing together the scattered legislation and offer better protection to the Indian investors. Accordingly, the Securities and Exchange Board of India (SEBI) was established on the 12th April, 1988. The Board was given the statutory status through an Ordinance Promulgated by the President of India on 31st January, 1992 which was later replaced by an Act of Parliament as the 4th April, 1992. SEBI with its over five years of existence has made considerable dent in the capital market through the various development and regulatory mechanism for investor protection and healthy development and regulation of the capital market.

But there are certain lapses in its functions which are mentioned below:

(a) SEBI has not attention on unauthorised trading houses (for the issue of corporate securities) coming up throughout the country. The recent episode M.S. Shoes company's case is a pertinent point where SEBI has lost its credibility on account of inefficiency of SEBI's officials.

(b) SEBI's guidelines are silent on the repercussions on market intermediates when they break the rules of share transactions.

References

1. Kannan, President, Investors' Association, Madras, South India.
2. V. Raghunathan, Business Today, Nov' 22-Dec' 6, 1993, p 119.

6

Analysis of Survey Data-I

The present study throws light on the key factors that affect primary market and also the factors responsible for the sluggish secondary market operation at present. The analysis is based on the responses elicited from sample stock market brokers, investors and professionals. In this process, the two groups of respondents (brokers - 25, professionals and investors - 75) were contacted and their views were obtained on the trading operations in the primary and secondary market, which were relevant for the study of investor protection through a questionnaire. The analysis of the survey data is presented in the following passages.

Primary Market

To find out the influential factors of the primary markets, the respondents were asked to rank any three factors among a list of factors that would affect trading activities in the primary market. The trading activities in primary market are governed under the provisions of SEBI Act, 1992. The weighted average score for all the factors was calculated and their ranks were taken into account. Kendall's concordance 'w' test was used to ascertain the views expressed by the two groups of respondents whether given a similar opinion about the trading operations (or) not. The following table shows the particulars of various factors taken up for the study.

TABLE III
Major Factors Affecting Primary Market with Rank

Factor	Rank
Pricing of premium issues	1
Inadequate disclosure of information	2
Over pricing of rights issues	3
Delay in allotment and issue of share certificates	4
Ineffective handling of the issues	5
Differential pricing for promoters	6
Stringent regulatory mechanism	7
Preferential allotment to foreign investors	8
Slackness of regulatory mechanism	9
Failure of issues in foreign market	10
Any other factor	11

Source: Primary Data

From the above table, it is clear that a maximum number of stock brokers, investors and professionals consider that pricing of premium issues is the very important factor that affects primary market at present. They feel that fixing of high premium on the shares by a large number of companies, even though their shares are not worth for such high premium affects the ordinary investors. Those capital issues which are worth can be issued at good premium. They have agreed that some issues fixed at premium are worth. The second important factor according to them which affects the primary market trading at present is the inadequate disclosure of information by the issuing companies. According to them, the issuing companies do not provide adequate information to the investors or they provide false information to them. This would affect the interest of the investors in general. And the third important factor that affects the primary market trading is over-pricing of rights issues. Today, rights issues are overpriced. This would again affect the shareholders who are going to subscribe to the rights issue.

Association in the Responses of Sharebrokers, Investors and Professionals

The survey data were further delved by dividing the respondents into two categories, i.e., share brokers on one side and investors and professionals on the other side to examine the association of their views. To find out consistency of opinion among the responses from the two different groups, Kendall's coefficient of concordance method was employed. The computed value of W is near 1 (Let us take the range as 0.86-1.05), which seems to indicate a strong similarity between the different sets of respondents[1].

Kendall has developed a technique which helps to determine the relationship between two or more sets of ranks[2]. To find out agreement between the ranks Kendall suggested a formula to determine the rank correlation coefficient.

$$\text{Kendall's coefficient of rank correlation} = \frac{12 \quad D^2}{m^2 (N) (N^2 - 1)}$$

$$\bar{x} = \frac{X}{N}$$

Where, m = Number of judges,

N = Number of factors,

D = Deviation between ranks.

Table III projects the details of computation of coefficient of concordance among the ranks in three important factors affecting the trading activities in primary market by two groups of respondents.

TABLE IV
Views of Different Categories of Respondents on Primary Market Trading

Factor	Rank				
	Stock Brokers R_1	Investors & Professionals R_2	X $R_1 + R_2$	D $X + \bar{x}$	D^2
Stringent regulatory mechanism	7	8	15	3	9
Slackness in regulatory mechanism	10	9	19	7	49
Differential pricing for promoters	6	4	10	-2	4
Pricing of premium issues	1	1	2	-10	100
Delay in allotment & issues of share certificates	2	5	7	-5	25
Preferential allotment to foreign investor	8	7	15	3	9
Over pricing of rights issue	5	2	7	-5	25
Ineffective handling of the issues	4	6	10	-2	4
Inadequate disclosure	3	3	6	-6	36
Failure of issues in foreign market	11	10	21	9	81
Any other factor	9	11	20	8	64
Total			132		406

Source: Primary Data

$$\text{Kendall's coefficient of rank correlation} = \frac{12 \quad D^2}{m^2 (N) (N^2 - 1)}$$

$m = 2, \quad D^2 = 406, \quad N = 12, \quad \bar{x} = \frac{132}{11} = 12$

$$= \frac{12 \quad 406}{2^2 \ (12) \ (12^2 - 1)}$$

$$= \frac{4872}{6864} = 0.71$$

Kendall's coefficient of rank correlation value = 0.71

It is observed that stock brokers consider that pricing of premium issues, delay in allotment and issues of share certificates and inadequate disclosure of information by issuing companies are the three major factors that affect primary market trading at present whereas investors/professionals feel that pricing of premium issues, over pricing of rights issues and inadequate disclosure of information by issuing companies are the three important factors that affect primary market trading. One could see from the above table that the two groups of respondents' order of importance differ. The calculated value of w is 0.71, which is less than 1. The views expressed by the two groups of respondents, namely, (stock brokers and investors/professionals) consider differently on this issue.

Secondary Market

To find out the influential factors that result in slackness in the secondary market, the respondents were asked to rank the first three important factors from a list of factors causing such sluggishness in the secondary market at present. The trading activities in secondary market are governed under the two statutes, namely, Securities Contracts (Regulation) Act, 1956, and SEBI Act, 1992. For this purpose, stock brokers, investors and professionals were contacted with a questionnaire and their responses were analysed. The weighted average scores for all the factors were calculated and their ranks analysed according to their importance. Kendall's concordance coefficient of rank correlation was used to find out association between the views expressed by the respondents for the secondary market factors and the ranks assigned by them. The results of the analysis of the survey data are incorporated in the following table:

TABLE V

Major Factors for Sluggish Secondary Market with Ranks

Factor	Rank
Operation of modified Badla system	1
Pessimism and lack of confidence	2
Delay in settlement of cash transaction	3
Restrictive regulation	4
Lack of & slow movement of funds	5
Mutual fund operations	6
Slackness in regulation	7
Operations of FIIS	8
Any other	9

Source: Primary Data

From the above table, it is clear that a maximum number of respondents consider that Operation of modified badla system is largely responsible for a sluggish secondary market. The second rank of pessimism and lack of confidence among investors regarding the rapid changes in the economy is found to be largely responsible for the sluggish secondary market. Investors are totally confused and not willing to invest in the secondary market and take risk rather, going to primary issues. Also they feel that delay in settlement of cash transactions is the third important factor in the secondary market at present.

It is worthwhile to mention that the respondents are divided into two groups, i.e, stock brokers on one side and investors and professionals on the other to know the differences in their views on this issue. The results of the analysis of the survey data in this regard are incorporated in the following table, and Kendall's coefficient of rank correlation was applied.

TABLE VI

Views of Different Categories of Respondents on Secondary Market

Factor	Rank				
	Share Brokers R_1	Investors & Professionals R_2	X $R_1 + R_2$	D $X + \bar{x}$	D^2
Operation of Modified Badla System	1	1	2	-8	64
Pessimism and lack of confidence	3	3	6	-4	16
Delay in settlement of cash transaction	6	2	8	-2	4
Restrictive regulation	7	7	14	4	16
Lack of & slow movement of funds	5	6	11	-1	1
Mutual fund operations	8	8	16	6	36
Slackness in regulation	2	4.5	6.5	-3.5	12.25
Operations of FIIS	4	4.5	8.5	-1.5	2.5
Any Other Factor	9	9	18	8	64
	Total		90		215.5

Source: Primary Data

$$\text{Kendall's coefficient of rank correlation} = \frac{12 \quad D^2}{m^2\ (N)\ (N^2 - 1)}$$

$$m = 2, \quad D^2 = 215.5, \quad N = 9, \quad x = \frac{90}{9} = 10$$

$$= \frac{12 \quad 215.5}{2^2\ (9)\ \ (9^2 - 1)} \quad \frac{2586}{2880} = 0.90$$

Kendall's coefficient of rank correlation value 0.90.

From the above table, it is observed that both the categories of respondents feel that Operation of modified badla system is the major factor. The calculated value is 0.90, which is nearly 1. It seems to indicate a strong similarity of opinion on the secondary market factors between the share brokers, and investors & professionals.

Summary

The study brings to limelight the key factors that affect trading in the primary market and the factors responsible for a sluggish secondary market. It is found that

1. Pricing of premium issues, Delay in allotment of shares and issue of share certificates, inadequate disclosure of information and overpricing of right issues are the important factors affecting the primary markets. Therefore, it is found from the analysis of the respondents' views based on their income, professional qualifications, investment conditions, trading conditions, that the innocent investors are adversely affected by the above factors. It indicates that in order to safeguard the interest of investors, primary market operations are to be regulated.
2. The analysis unveils that in the secondary market operation of modified badla system, pessimism and lack of confidence among investors and delay in settlement of cash transactions are the important factors responsible for a sluggish secondary market. In this connection, the

innocent investors are to be safeguarded by granting more powers to SEBI to supervise effectively the secondary market operations.

References

1. LYMANOTT, Study guide for statistics – A tool for the social sciences, (3rd pt), 1974, edition, p. 136.
2. N M Downie and R W Health, Basic Statistical Methods, Harper International Edition, New York, 1970, p. 25.

7

Analysis of Survey Data-II

Introduction

In this chapter, the matters connected with insider trading, pricing of securities, badla system, futures and options, investors' protection measures are examined. These activities are governed under the Securities Contracts (Regulation) Act, 1956 and SEBI Act, 1992. Based on the respondents' age, income, professional qualification, investment in the securities and trading in the market, these matters were analysed by applying five point scale.

Insider Trading

"INSIDER means any person who, is or was connected with the company or is deemed to have been connected with the company, and who is reasonably expected to have access, by virtue of such connection, to unpublished price sensitive information in respect of securities of the company, or who has received or has had access to such unpublished price sensitive information"[1]-SEBI.

A person who, because of his or her position within a firm, has access to proprietary information unavailable to the general public is called insider. Such insider's trade in the securities market, is called insider trading, i.e., the illegal buying or selling of securities on the basis of information that is generally unavailable to the general public is called insider trading. An example is the purchase by a Director of shares of his or her firm's stock just before the release of surprisingly good earnings information. Although the term insider obviously includes corporate officers, it also may extend to relatives of these officers or to employees of other firms having a special relationship with the firm in question. Officially, an officer, Director or the owner of 10% or more of a firm's securities is called an insider. In the definition given by SEBI, the following explanations are being given:–

Connected Person

"Connected Person" means any person who (i) is a Director, as defined in clause (13) of Section 2 of the Companies Act, 1956, or is deemed to be a Director of that company by virtue of sub-clause (10) of section 307 of that Act, or (ii) occupies the position of an officer or an employee of the company or holds a position involving a professional or business relationship between himself and the company and who may reasonably be expected to have an access to unpublished price sensitive information in relation to that company[2].

Deemed to have been Connected

A person deemed to be a connected person if such person

(i) is a company under the same management of group or any subsidiary company thereof within the meaning of Section (1b) of Section 370, or Sub-section (11) of Section 372, of the Companies Act, 1956 (1 of 1956) or sub-clause (9) of Section 2 of the MRTP Act, 1969 (54 of 1969) as the case may be; or

(ii) is an official or a member of a stock exchange or of a clearing house of that stock exchange, or a dealer in securities within the meaning of clause (c) of section 2, and section 17 of the Securities Contracts (Regulations) Act, 1956 (42 of 1956) respectively or any employee of such member or dealer of a stock exchange;

(iii) is a merchant banker, share transfer agent, Registrar to an issue, debenture trustee, broker, portfolio manager, investment advisor, sub-broker, investment company or an employee thereof, or is a member of the Board of Trustees of a mutual fund or a member of the Board of Directors of the asset management company of a mutual fund or is an employee thereof who have a fiduciary relationship with the company;

(iv) is a member of the Board of Directors, or an employee, of a public financial institution as defined in Section 4A, of the companies Act, 1956; or

(v) is an official or an employee of a self regulatory organisation recognised or authorised by the Board of a regulatory body; or

(vi) is a relative of any of the afore mentioned persons;

(vii) is a banker of the company.

Unpublished Price Sensitive Information

"Unpublished price sensitive information" means any information which relates to the following matters or is of concern, directly or indirectly, to a company, and is not generally known or published by such company for general information, but which if published or known, is likely to materially affect the price of securities of that company in the market. Such information includes

(i) financial results (both half-yearly and annual) of the company;

(ii) intended declaration of dividends (both interim and final);

(iii) issue of shares by way of public rights and bonus;

(iv) any major expansion plans or execution of new projects;

(v) amalgamations, mergers and take-overs;

(vi) disposed of the whole or substantially the whole of the undertaking;

(vii) such other information as may affect the earnings of the company;

(viii) any changes in policies, plans or operations of the company.

Securities and Exchange Board of India has issued guidelines for prohibition of insider trading and also for effective investigation into the cases of insider trading. These regulations may be called Securities and Exchange Board of India (Insider Trading) Regulations, 1992. Based on the regulations, no insider shall

(i) either on his own behalf or on behalf of any other person, deal in securities of a company listed on any stock exchange on the basis of any unpublished price sensitive information;

(ii) communicate any unpublished price sensitive information to any person, with or without his request for such information, except as required in the ordinary course of business or under any law; or

(iii) counsel or procure any other person to deal in securities of any company on the basis of unpublished price sensitive information.

Any insider who deals in securities or communicates any information or counsels any person dealing in securities in contravention of the provisions or regulations of the SEBI Act shall be guilty of insider trading.

During the study, an attempt was made to find out the views of respondents on insider trading. In this regard, stock brokers, investors, and professionals' responses were obtained through a interview schedule on insider trading. There were six statements regarding insider trading in the interview schedule issued to the respondents. Their views were recorded on a five point scale. The average score of respondents for these statements was calculated. The table given below shows the mean scores of respondents on insider trading.

TABLE VII
Mean Scores on Insider Trading

Statement	Mean Scores
Insider Trading:-	
1. is a regular feature	3.8100
2. occurs on certain specific occasions	3.8000
3. is harmful to the market	4.1200
4. provides undue advantage to certain traders	4.2600
5. present regulatory mechanism is adequate to control	2.9000
6. SEBI's regulations are inadequate to prevent and control	3.4300

Source: Primary Data.

From the above analysis, it is clear that on a five point scale the stock brokers, investors, and professionals consider that insider trading is a regular feature and it occurs on certain specific occasions like issue of shares and convertible debentures of listed companies only. They have strongly agreed that it is harmful to the market and it provides undue advantage to certain traders over others. Most of them have disagree with the statement that the present regulatory mechanism is adequate to control the insider trading, but have clearly expressed that SEBI's regulations are absolutely inadequate to prevent and control insider trading in Indian stock markets. They are in favour of a strong regulatory mechanism from SEBI.

During the study, an attempt was made to analyse the difference in the opinion within the group of share brokers and investors with the age, income, qualification, investment in securities and trading in the market as the criteria. The results are incorporated in the following table:

TABLE VIII

Mean Squares and 'F' Prob

Criteria	Mean Square	'F' Prob
Age	0.4380	0.3745
Income	1.3040	0.0318
Professional qualification	0.1410	0.5715
Investment in securities	3.7453	0.0031
Trading in market	3.9947	0.0022

Source : Primary Data.

It is observed that if income, investment in securities and trading in the market are taken as criteria, there is significant difference in them as regards insider trading. It means, high income group and low income group, those who invest in securities and those who do not, those who often trade in the securities market and those who do not, consider differently regarding the insider trading. But if age and professional qualification are taken as the criteria, there is no significant difference in their views. It means respondents in all age groups, and those professionally qualified and those not professionally qualified feel alike regarding the insider trading. Therefore, the difference in opinion on insider trading is due to income of the respondents, and their investment status in the securities or trading status in the market.

Pricing of Securities

The Securities and Exchange Board of India has issued new guidelines for capital issues following the abolition of the Controller of Capital Issues Act. The new guidelines give existing listed companies full freedom to price their capital issues in consultation with the lead managers. Existing private limited and closely held companies have been giving pricing freedom provided they have a three year track record of consistent profitability. In the case of entirely new issues, an entrepreneur without a track record can issue capital only at par. Where the new company is set up by an existing company with a five year track record of consistent profitability, it will be free to fix its issue price subject to certain restrictions under SEBI Act.

There is a general tendency among the investors, that because of the abolition of the Controller of Capital Issues Act (CCI), pricing of premium issues is high as also the prices of rights issues. There is a general tendency that the market prices of the securities do not reflect the true worth of securities and also the CCI method of pricing the premium issues. In regard to the market price of the security, there is a general feeling that it is absolutely possible to influence the price by unfair means. To analyse all the issues in the pricing of securities, the views of stock brokers, investors and professionals were obtained with the help of the interview schedule. Their responses on pricing of securities, and the differences in their views, if any, are presented here. There were nine statements regarding pricing of securities and the views of respondents were recorded on a five point scale. The average score of respondents for these statements is provided in the following table.

TABLE IX
Mean Scores on Pricing of Securities

Statement	Mean Score
Pricing of Securities:	
1. Market prices reflect true worth	2.9100
2. Demand and supply that determine the price	2.3000
3. Possible to influence the price by unfair means	3.8900
4. Premium issue is fair and acceptable	2.9200
5. Premium issue pricing method is fair and acceptable	2.8200
6. Justification for premium issue is vague and inadequate	3.4300
7. Rights issues are unduly high	3.9500
8. Differential pricing is required and justified	2.3300
9. CCI method is to be made mandatory	2.0800

Source: Primary Data.

It is evident from the above table the stock brokers, investors, professionals consider that market prices of the securities, reflect the true worth of securities and have strongly agreed that it is possible to influence the price of a security by unfair means. Very few have agreed that it is demand and supply that determine the security price. A number of them are of the view that apart from the demand and supply there are other significant factors that also play a role in the determination of the security prices.

Though there is a general feeling that pricing of premium issues is high, stock brokers, investors and professionals consider that the premium issues is fair and acceptable. But few of the respondents are of the view that the premium issues are high, and the method of pricing of premium issue is not fair and also not acceptable. But, a majority of respondents have agreed that the method of pricing of premium issues is fair and acceptable, and have strongly agreed that the justification for the fixation of pricing of premium issues is vague and inadequate.

A large number of respondents are of the view that the prices of rights issue are unduly high. In recent years, the rights issues are high and the investors consider it is difficult to pay the unduly high prices for rights issues. The respondents are against the differential pricing of securities and they have felt that CCI method for pricing premium issue is not to be made mandatory. During the study, an attempt was made to examine the views within the two groups, namely, stock broker on the one side and the investors and professionals on the other side with the age, income, qualification, investment status in securities and trading status in the market as criteria. The analysis of the survey data in this regard is shown in the table placed underneath.

TABLE X

Mean Squares and 'F' Prob

Criteria	Mean square	'F' Prob
Age	0.2510	0.3729
Income	0.1813	0.5547
Professional qualification	0.4588	0.1799
Investment in securities	0.4739	0.1713
Trading in market	0.2818	0.2924

Source: Primary Data.

It is observed that if age, income, professional qualification, investment in securities and trading in the market are taken as criteria, there is no significant difference in their views as regards pricing of securities. It means the respondents in the different age groups, monthly income groups, professionally qualified and not qualified, often traded and often not traded agree that it is possible to influence price of a security by unfair means.

Operation of Modified Badla System

Bull is an operator who first buys and then sells shares on the assumption that the prices will go up in the near future. Badla transaction is one in which the bull operator purchases shares on borrowed money for which he pays interest[3]. The money is borrowed from one account day to the next account day, i.e., for the period of one settlement. This is also called contango. Contango charges depend on the ruling rate of market interests and the quantum of purchase position in the shares sought to be carried over from one settlement to the other.

Badla charges are the interest payable for the period of carry over of purchase/sale positions from one settlement to the other for the value of the shares. Normally, badla charges are paid up by the buyers to the sellers, as the buyer retains his funds with him without taking delivery of the shares bought, and such funds would normally earn some interests, based on market rates of interest. It is for this reason badla charges are usually payable by buyers. In unusual conditions of the market, where there is a heavy over selling in certain shares and sellers are not able to tender delivery of the documents, the sellers may be called upon to pay to the buyers the badla charges and many sellers wish to carry over this positions. Such badla charges are called 'backwardation or Undha Badla'.

Contracts for the "clearing", popularly known as forward trading, were prohibited by the Government of India on the 27th June, 1969. This led to a prolonged lull in the stock market activities which improved only when trading for hand delivery contracts were divided into two categories, viz., 'A' group and 'B' group. A type of trading was evolved in the 'A' group which conformed ostensibly to the definition of a hand the delivery contract, viz., for delivery and payment within fourteen days following from one cycle of trading of fourteen days to another by paying badla charges.

For such specified shares, there were a strict schedule of regulatory measures like automatic daily margins, carry-over margins, ad-hoc margins, limits on holdings of individual members and limits on the outstanding position in the market. Implementation of these regulatory measures has been strictly monitored by the stock exchange authorities. The system of trading in specified shares was worked quite satisfactorily.

For carrying forward the transaction from the current settlement period to the next settlement period, the buyer normally pays seller a consideration called contango charge (badla) which is fixed by the market force in the open market badla session. The buyer makes badla purely on his own volition. It is because some of the buyers do not want to take delivery and the seller does not have the shares, the buyer can demand consideration known as backwardation charges or Undha badla. It is also open to a buyer to refuse to receive Undha badla and insist on delivery in which case the stock exchange administration automatically moves in and effects the auction at the cost and risk of the defaulting seller.

The existence of modified badla facility can be used for hedging the stocks held by an investor against any likely fall in prices. This is often also resorted to when shares are sent to the company for transfer or sub-division into trading lots. The hedge facility is also availed of by holders of convertible debentures against the shares arising out of conversion. Those anticipating the flow of funds in future can avail of the badla facility as a hedge against the rise in price. The badla financier uses the badla facility as a means of temporary finance by holders of shares by making teji badla, i.e., selling in the current settlement and receiving payment against the sales and buying in the next settlement – a process which can be repeated after every settlement till the need for finance lasts. As banks finance securities upto only 50% of the ruling market price being lent, badla acts not merely as a hedge instrument but also as a source of both investment and finance.

Merits and Demerits

The Badla is an almost perfect hedge instrument[4]. The question of any lack of correlation between futures and spot prices detracting the instrument from acting as a perfect hedge does not just exist. There is also no question of payment of any premium amount as the market is equally balanced between the buyer and the seller. Payment of contango by the buyer to the seller, is only by way of interest on the price of the shares bought by him but not paid for.

Liquidity in a share having badla facility is much higher than in a share without the badla facility. The increase in liquidity is also accompanied by reduced volatility. Studies have revealed that while the annual average range of fluctuations of some select shares in the specified groups is about 50%. the corresponding figure for the most active in the non-specified group is about

65%. In addition, the spreads in specified shares are not more than 1.5% while the spreads in the non-specified share are generally over 5%. The average spreads in specified shares at the Bombay Stock Exchange (BSE) are about 1% while spreads in respect of the most active stocks on the London Stock Exchange are about 2%.

Specified shares have an inherent buoyant component because of the facility of carry-over. Whenever a share is transferred from the non-specified group of specified group, its prices rise instantly and vice-versa.

Badla is often accused of lack of transparency. This is no longer true. The BSE publishes on a daily basis the outstanding business in each strip. The names of the top ten members carrying forward outstanding sale and purchases positions as also aggregate of outstanding sale and purchase positions from one settlement cycle to another are now given with details. Whatever further information is required in this regard can and should be published. Any time lag in the flow of the information is only because of the present stage of development of automation and will affect futures and options as well.

Whatever may be the merits and demerits of badla system, it was banned by the Government of India and SEBI in the year 1994. But now they have introduced modified badla system. An attempt was made during the survey to analyse the stock brokers, investors, and professionals' views on this issue. Relevant questions were framed on this issue and the related responses were recorded with the help of a interview schedule. These questions arranged in the of statements, and responses recorded on a five point scale are presented in the table given below:

TABLE XI

Mean Scores on Operation of Modified Badla Systems

Statement	Mean Score
Badla system	
1. is harmful to the market	3.5400
2. should be banned	305100
3. helps in stabilising the market	3.4400
4. regulations are adequate and required	2.9800
5. restrictions are inadequate	3.1300

Source: Primary Data.

From the results given above, it is clear that the stock brokers, investors and professionals consider that badla system has helped in stabilising the market and it should be banned; 40% of the respondents have agreed that badla system helps in stabilising the market and have also supported that the regulations are required, but they are of the view that restrictions on the system are inadequate with reference to the modified badla system. It is found that in regard to operation for modified badla system, there is no difference among the views of the stock brokers, investors, and professionals.

Further probe into the difference in the responses on operation of modified badla system with reference to respondents of different age groups, income groups, professionally qualified and those not qualified, investment status in the securities and trading in the market, was made. The results are given in the following table.

TABLE XII

Mean Squares and 'F' Prob

Criterion	Mean Square	'F' Prob
Age	2.4115	0.0353
Income	0.9949	0.2658
Professional qualification	2.5198	0.0636
Investment in securities	0.6402	0.3522
Trading in market	1.1537	0.2108

Source: Primary Data.

From the analysis of responses, it is found that if age, income, professional qualification, investment in securities and trading status in the market are taken as criteria, there is no significant difference in the views of respondents as regards the existence of modified Badla system. It means that whether high income group or low income group, or those who are professionally qualified or not, or those who invest in the securities or not, and those who often trade in the market have agreed that SEBI's regulations on modified badla system have to seriously consider about the protection of investors' in the stock exchanges.

Futures and Options

A future contract is like a forward contract and is a binding agreement to buy or sell a specified quantity of a commodity on a specified future date at a price agreed upon when the agreement is entered into[5]. The above definition describes a commodity future; in the case of a financial future, the specified commodity is a financial instrument. Therefore, a financial future is an agreement to buy or sell, a standard quantity of a financial investment or foreign currency at a future date at an agreed price.

The main difference between future contracts and forward contracts are as follows:-

★ While forward markets are OTC markets, the futures are traded in organised futures exchanges with the sale and purchases being struck in the trading pits of such exchanges.

★ The contract for the forward purchase or sale is between the buyer and the seller; in futures trading, as in the case of options trading, the clearing house interposes itself between the buyer and seller.

★ To enter into a futures contract, say, purchase of a future contract, the investor has to deposit a specified percentage of a current value of the securities as margin money with the exchange. The exchange will mark the margin to the contract on a daily basis. That is, if the market price of the security rises above a certain percentage, the exchange will call for additional margin and if the market price falls below a certain percentage, the excess margin will be refunded or placed at the credit of the investor.

Stock Index Futures

Though various classes of futures contracts such as commodity futures, currency futures, interest rate futures and stock index features are traded in the well developed countries, here only stock index futures and some of the hedging strategies that are possible with them are discussed.

A stock index futures contract is an obligation to deliver at settlement an amount of cash equal to 500 time (or any such multiple) the difference between the stock index value at the close of the last trading day of the contract, and the price at which the futures contract was originally struck. Under the stock index futures contract, no physical delivery of shares can be made. Both the buyer and the seller would have to deposit margins which typically vary between 5% ad 10% of the value of the contract. The value of the contract is the index value of the futures contract multiplied, by the specified multiple. Trading in futures contracts at all these exchanges is confined to indices and does not extend to individual scrips.

While innumerable strategies may be devised which involve the use of the stock index futures, here only two simple strategies are considered. They are (1) Anticipatory hedge and (2) Short hedge.

(1) Anticipatory Hedge

This strategy can be best explained with the help of an example. Suppose "X" expects to receive Rs. 8,00,000 from the maturity of a deposit after six months, Hence, he wishes to invest this amount in certain blue chips included in the calculation of sensitivity index. X is worried, however, that the prices of the securities may rise in the six month interval and Rs. 8,00,000 may not be sufficient to buy the quantities that he has planned to buy. To hedge against this possibility, X may buy one six- month sensitivity index futures contract at Rs 2,800. The expectation is that if share prices appreciate, the increased value of the futures contract will offset the higher acquisition cost. Suppose that at the end of six-months, the sensitivity index moves to Rs. 3000, X gains Rs. 200 (Rs. 3000-Rs.2800) on the futures contract. Consider that the acquisition cost of shares he has planned to buy has moves up by 10%, that is, the total acquisition cost of shares is Rs.8,80,000. Through the hedging strategy, X would have funds to meet the increased cost of acquisition and also have a surplus of Rs. 20,000.

Short Hedge

This hedging strategy suits an investor having a portfolio of shares which he intends to hold for a long-term. However, the investor anticipates that in the next few months, the market may face rough weather and as a consequence, the share prices would tumble down. Instead of selling his current portfolio, the investor can sell an index futures contract short. If the actual decline in the index is higher than the level of index indicated in the contract, the investor stands to gain and thus the gain to compensate the notional loss suffered on the portfolio.

Options

An option may be defined as "an agreement between two parties under which the option buyers acquire the right to buy or sell a specified period of time at a specified price regardless of the market price security. An option contract confers upon its holder the right to buy or sell an underlying instrument at a agreed price during a specific time period. The holder (buyer) of options has rights but not obligations while the writer (seller) of options has obligations but no rights[6].

Following are the some of the features and terms used in option contracts:

★ For an option contract to come into existence, two parties are essential – the option buyer and the option seller, the latter is also referred to as the writer of the option.

★ If the option contract confers the right on the option buyer to buy some specified securities, then the option is referred to as a call option. An option under which the buyers can exercise the right to sell is known as a put option.

★ The price at which the securities can be brought/sold under the contract is known as the exercise price or the striking price.

★ Though the buyer of an option has the right to buy/sell, he has no obligation to buy/sell. In other words, an option may expire without any purchase or sale of securities. However, the option writer is obliged to sell when the buyer exercises his right to buy and viceversa. Thus, only the buyer of the option really has an option.

★ The option contract must specify an expiration date. If the option can be exercised at any time on or before the expiration date then such an option is known as American option. An European option can be exercised only on the expiration date specified in the contract.

★ For the obligation that the option writer undertakes, the buyer pays a compensation which is referred to as the price of the option or premium. This premium ranges between 5% to 30% of the market value of the security underlying the option.

There are call option and put option. A call option gives its owner the right to buy the underlying instrument at a pre-determined price known as the strike price while a put option is a contract that gives its owner the right to sell the underlying instrument at a pre-determined price, i.e., the strike price. The buyer of the option has to pay the option seller, the option premium, which is determined by the market forces.

There are option contracts not only in respect of individual stocks but also on stock index and stock index futures. The differences between the two is that while in case of individual stocks, delivery of shares is taken at the strike price, in the case of index and index futures, there will be only cash settlement between the value of the index and its strike price multiplied by the size of the standardised contract. Options can be used as hedges against a fall in the price of owned stocks by either writing a call option or by buying a put option.

Hedging through options is relatively costlier because of the premium the option buyers has to pay. Studies in advanced countries reveal that turnover increases in the underlying shares of those companies in respect of which options have launched. It is, not clear whether the increase in turnover has led to any decline in volatility options stimulate speculation.

During the present study, the stock brokers, investors and professionals' views on the operations of futures and options and the new investments' avenue. Relevant questions framed on this issue were collected through interview schedule and these were arranged in the form of statements; and the study participants responses were recorded on a five point scale. A portrait of the statements and their mean scores is laid in the following table.

TABLE XIII

Means Score on Futures and Options

Statement	Mean Score
Futures and Options	
1. a better alternative	2.7200
2. to be introduced cautiously	1.5700
3. no need as the present system is satisfactory	2.6800

Source: Primary Data.

It can be seen that on a five point scale the stock brokers, investors and professionals consider that futures and options provide a better alternative to the present modified badla system and think that there is no need to delay the introduction of this alternative. At the same time, some other respondents' consider that there is no need to introduce futures and options as the present modified badla system is satisfactory.

An attempt was made to analyse the opinions within the two groups, namely, stock brokers, investment professionals with age, income, qualification, investment status in securities, and trading in the market, taken as criteria. The results are captured in the table furnished hereunder :

TABLE XIV

Mean Square and "F" Prob

Criteria	Mean Square	"F" Prob
Age	0.8301	0.1145
Income	1.2771	0.0168
Professional Qualification	0.4710	0.2637
Investment in Securities	0.206	0.532
Trading in the Market	0.2502	0.4223

Source: Primary Data

The foregoing analysis reveals that if age, income, professional qualification, investment in securities and trading in the market are taken as criteria, there is no significant difference between the views of the stock brokers, and investors and professionals regarding the operations of futures and options. That is to say, the respondents in all age groups, income group, those who are professionally qualified and those who are not, those who invest in the securities and those who do not, those who often trade in the security market and those who do not often trade consider that futures and options system provide better alternative to the modified badla system. However, the slackness in the futures and options system are to be set right through SEBI's regulations. It is clear from the foregoing discussion that the trading activities such as insider trading, badla system and futures and options are governed by the provisions of the Securities Contract (Regulation) Act, 1956 and SEBI Act, 1992.

Investors' Protection Measures

SEBI has been receiving investors' complaints directly since its inception[7]. SEBI has introduced an automated compliants handling system to deal with these complaints. To create an awareness among the issuers and intermediaries of the need to redress investors' grievances quickly, SEBI has been issuing fortnightly press releases publishing the names of the erring companies and this acts as a constraint in the direct redressal of the investors' grievances. SEBI has therefore been taking up these complaints with the Department of Company Affairs which has the power vested under it by the Companies Act for redressal of the grievances.

Delay in posting of refund orders in the case of oversubscribed issues, is one of the major complaints of investors applying for public issues. To help the investors in this matter, SEBI has introduced an additional facility called stockinvest. The investors can use this instrument in applying for public and right issues. The advantage to the investors lies in the nature of instrument because the investor's account in his own bank get debited only when he has received an allotment. The[7] investor's money therefore remains in the account till allotment and earns interest. SEBI has taken a number of measures to smoothen the procedures involved in the use of the instrument. Delays in registration and transfer of securities are also the major compliants of the investors. SEBI has been taking up such compliants with the Department of Company Affairs, so that stringent action is taken against erring companies. To ensure that no malpractices take place in the allotment process in oversubscribed public issues, SEBI has appointed its representatives to supervise the allotment process. Investors Associations which have been established at different parts of the country can become agents for creating a greater awareness among investors. SEBI has given recognition to several genuine, active investors' associations, geographically diversified and supports their activities in different ways. To enlighten investors on various issues relating to the securities market and of their rights and remedies, SEBI issues advertisements for investor guidance from time to time. Eight advertisements have been issued so far by SEBI. At the instance of SEBI, the stock exchanges have amended the listing agreements to provide for deposit of one percent of the issues amounts of a company making public issue. This amount deposited with the stock exchanges could be released only after the stock exchanges satisfy themselves that the issuers have taken all action particularly those related to dispatch of allotment letters and returned orders. This action on the part of SEBI has given the stock exchange an increased ability to redress the investor's grievances.

SEBI has issued several investors' guidance series measures for educating the investors. One of them is the "Factors to be considered for investment in the primary market". This investors' guidance series is intended to educate the investors about certain aspects which they normally should look for in the Memorandum containing salient features of prospectus accompanying all application forms, before making investment in any issue. For any further details relating to the issue, they should make a reference to the detailed prospectus which is available with the company or the merchant bankers managing the issue.

The investors should know the companies' history before making an investment. Hence the following are essential information to be noted by the investor.

1. Promoters Track Record

Adequacy of knowledge and experience in the field relating to the project, past performance of the companies promoted by them and their track record, and their reputation and integrity as promoters assessed by financial newspapers and magazines.

2. Professional Management

The Managing Director's background and experience in the field and composition the Board of Directors.

3. Objects of the Issue

Whether the purpose of the issue is likely to result in enhancement of the profitability and growth of the company.

4. Project details including location and raw materials.
5. Details regarding the product, technology used and the market of the product.
6. Financial data and profitability projections.
7. Pricing policy and pending litigation, if any.
8. Risk factors to ascertain specific risks and general risks related to the project.
9. Auditor's report and recent working results.
10. Statutory, institutional and bank dues, if any.
11. Statutory clearance required for the implementation of the project have been obtained or not.
12. Record of servicing of inquires from shareholders and investors.

In this context stock brokers, investors and professionals' views on the significance of investors' protection were obtained with the aid of a interview schedule. These questions were framed as statements to record and analyse the responses of the respondents. These statements and their means scores are tabulated as shown below:

TABLE XV

Mean Scores on Investor Protection

Statement	Mean Score
Small Investors	
1. being eased out of the market	4.1300
2. present ceiling is required	3.0400
3. present legal system provides enough safeguards	3.2800
4. have adequate opportunity for participation in security investment	3.0400

Source: Primary Data

The above investigation lays open that on a five point scale the stock brokers, investors and professionals consider that small investors are definitely eased out of stock market but stressed that the present ceiling on investment by small investor is required. They are of the view that the present legal system provides enough safeguards to small investors especially after SEBI's investors' protection measures, and agreed that small investors have adequate opportunities for participation in security investment in the market.

An attempt was made to analyse the difference in opinions within the two groups of respondents, namely, stock brokers and professionals/investors' with reference to their age, income, qualification, investment status in the securities, and trading status in the market. The results are shown in the following table:

TABLE XVI

Mean Squares and 'F' Prob.

Criteria	Mean Square	'F' Prob.
Age	0.2690	0.6777
Income	0.4607	0.5811
Professional qualification	0.1469	0.6372
Investment in securities	6.4453	0.0017
Trading in the market	1.2472	0.1770

Source: Primary Data

From the analysis of responses, it is observed that, the respondents in the different age groups, monthly income groups, professionally qualified, and not qualified, often traded and often not traded, have agree that SEBI' s investor protection measures have to seriously consider about the protection of investors' in the stock exchanges.

Summary

The matters examined in this chapter are insider trading, pricing of securities, modified badla system, futures and options and the significance of investors' protection. The respondents were requested to express their views on those issues on a five point scale by preparing certain specific statements on each of these system. Again analyses are made to see that there is any difference in their opinion due to age, income, professional qualification, investment status in the securities and trading in the market. To analyse all these, 'F' test is used. Statements on each system are analysed by calculating the mean scores and the results are presented. It is found that the activities of the stock market such as insider trading, modified badla system, futures and options are governed by the two statutes namely, Securities Contract (Regulation) Act, 1956 and SEBI Act, 1992. In this connection the innocent investors are to be safeguarded by granting more powers to SEBI to regulate the stock market activities.

References

1. SEBI (Insider Trading) Regulations, 1992.
2. David L. Scott, Wall Street Words, Hongton Mifflin Company, 1988, p. 176.
3. Indian Overseas Bank (IOB), Monthly News Review, June 1992, p. 14.
4. M.R. Mayya, Chartered Financial Analyst Journal, February 1994, p. 8.
5. Kalyani Ramachandran, Journal of Chartered Financial Analyst, August 1992, p. 9.
6. Kalyani Ramachandran, Chartered Financial Analyst, Jul-Aug. 1992, p.3.
7. "National Investor Awareness Programme", The Hindu, Madras, September 9, 1994, p. 14.

8

Investors' Services

It is explicit that the enactments like Companies Act, 1956, Securities Contracts (Regulation) Act, 1956 and SEBI Act, 1992 contain provisions to protect the interests of investors. However, they have not served the purpose fully. Hence, the investors must be aware of the other measures available for their protection. These measures are examined in this chapter. Fig. 8.1 portrays the significance of Investor's Services meant for Investors' protection.

It is a known fact that, the capital market in India has grown manifold in the last five to seven years. However, when compared to the western countries, it is still in its infant stage. The experts in the capital market predict a faster growth of the market coupled with a substantial increase in the number of investors. As already stated in Chapter III of this report, the investors are likely to have grievances. The investors' grievances must be redressed and they should be assured of prompt, efficient and reliable services to protect their interest. In this context, they should be aware of these services.

On their part, the companies to have taken the investors' problem seriously so much so that they have changed their earlier stand of having a centralised department for investors' problems in favour of giving the whole portfolio to outside specialised agencies as transfer agents. There is a growing awareness now that the handling of investors' problems is a specialised subject and if they fail to deliver efficient services, their chances to mobilise fresh

FIGURE 8.1
Significance of Investors' Services Meant for Investors' Protection

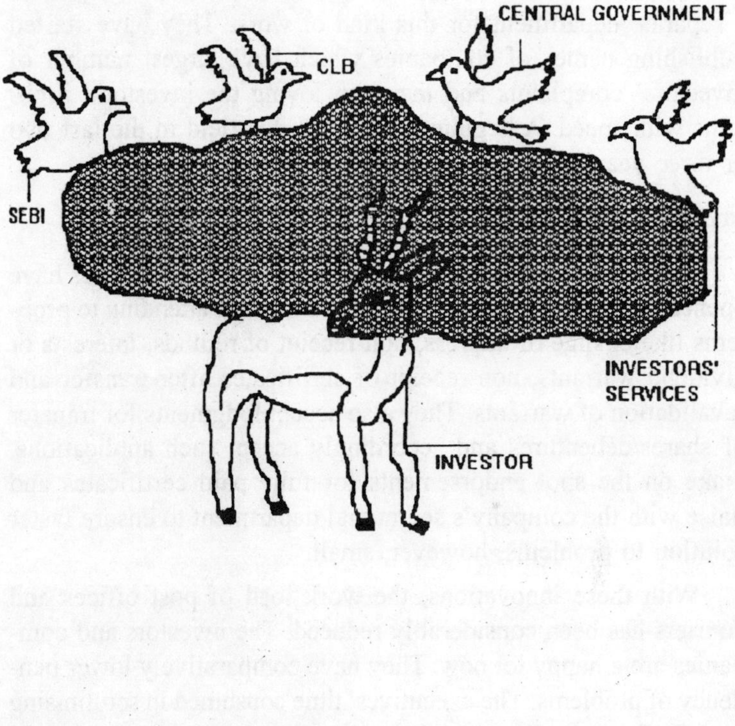

The Govt. alone cannot afford full support to the investor, but also the investors' services.

resources by way of public rights issue may be jeopardised, and eventually losing sympathy of investors.

The Government of India, also appreciating the fact that good investors' service is one of the important factors for a sound and healthy capital market, has started a service dialogue on this issue and has given powers to Securities and Exchange Board of India (SEBI) and stock exchanges for speedy redressals. In fact, both SEBI and stock exchanges have successfully launched a separate department for this kind of work. They have started publishing names of companies which have largest number of investors' complaints and insist on loving the investors' problems with speed. A beginning made in this field in the last two or three years is now gaining momentum.

Investors' Service Centre

Companies with lakhs of shareholders/debentureholders have opened permanent investors' service centres for attending to problems like change of address, non-receipt of refunds, interests or dividend warrants, non-receipt of certificates after transfer and revalidation of warrants. They also accept lodgments for transfer of shares/debentures and accordingly accept such applications, make on the spot endorsements for fully paid certificates and liaise with the company's secretarial department to ensure faster solution to problems, however, small.

With these innovations, the work load of post offices and couriers has been considerably reduced. The investors and companies are a happy lot now. They have comparatively lower pendency of problems. The executives' time consumed in scrutinising transfer forms has been minimised now as they are to check only the specimen signature and prepare a list of transfers for the Board meeting. With communication facilities improving, time is not far when all formalities relating to the transfer would be completed locally, and the local centre would send only the final list of transfer application for the Board to discuss and resolve. Such service centre in India where illiteracy level is high, help in narrowing the communication gaps as also overcoming linguistic barriers. Companies headquartered in Delhi may have a shareholder from a very remote village in Kerala State who may not be good at writing complaint in Hindi.* This sometimes becomes a major impediment in prompt redressal of grievances. The Reliance Industries Limited is one company which has opened such centres at many places in the country which have fared well. Opening of temporary investors' service centres for taking care of sudden increase in problems (especially after the closure of mega issues and their allotment) is also helpful, for instance, due to sudden spurt in the problems, it helps better understanding and faster solution of complaints. The Oswal Agro group is a company which had, at the time of mega-issue of Bindal Agro Chem. Ltd., opened such centres. Similarly, ICICI and Tata Timken Ltd., have also extended such facilities, although for a very short period, and for a very limited purpose of public issue complaints.

Lodegment Centres for Rights Issue

The application forms of rights issue which, hitherto were being accepted by banks are (in some cases) now being accepted at the predesignated company's service centre. In a few cases, the companies have decided to handle the acceptance of rights application form themselves. The bank's job would then be reduced to clearing of cheques and maintaining the collection account in terms of funds. This procedure ensures a perfect and better investors' assistance at the time of filling up the form, fewer rejections of forms, speedy clearing of cheques, faster remittances of funds and immediate allotment on closure of the issue. Earlier, the banks used to take longer time in processing the forms and thus the procedure of finalising the allotment entailed undue delay. Rights issues generally remain open for a month and the forms are relatively lesser than public issues. As a consequence of this, the banks were taking their own time to finalise the processing before arriving at the final collection figure. This system was followed by TELCO, Deepak Nitrate, Procter and Gamble, Ashok Leyland, Ranbaxy, Nicholas Lab., ESAB India, Indian Organic and so forth. The indicators for future

* Native language in northern parts of India.

events are that the companies may resort to such arrangements in relation to collection of allotment and call money and may also consider lodgement of public issue forms at private investors' service centres. This would, however, require a clear cut legislation[1].

The question is, can a private service centre provide as good or as strong an infrastructure as a bank can? The bankers have the advantage to pool a large contingent of staff when suddenly required, it would have the necessary space also and generally speaking it can cope with a large volume of work. The private service centre may initially face problems in building up the requisite infrastructure.

Lodgement of Debenture Certificates of Redemption

This is smaller to lodgements to buy-back. The debenture-holders are requested to lodge certificates along with advance stamped receipt at the predesignated centres throughout the country. The holders are then sent redemption amount by pay orders. This avoids inconvenience for the investors, ensures proper filling up of form and saves postal authorities of work.

Specific Centre for on the Spot Endorsement for Call Money Paid

A few companies have started giving on the spot endorsement (as fully paid) facility at local service centres. This process hardly takes a few minutes. It facilitates the investors in transacting on the share certificates which he is holding, thereby saving the agency of waiting for a month after sending them to the company for the endorsements.

It is time for the Government to insist on companies with very large shareholders base to open full time permanent service centres, not only in four metros in India but also at all places where stock exchanges function. One of the objectives of granting legislation to SEBI was to inspire confidence in investors and protecting their interests. The recent guidelines and code of conduct also require the stock exchange members to modernise investment services, introduce better and innovative practices in the interest of investors. In this context, it is apt to mention the SEBI's achievement for the redressal of investors' grievances.

Redressal of Investors' Grievances by SEBI

In an effort to improve the quality of intermediatry services available to investors, procedures have been instituted for redressal of investors' grievances arising from the issue procedure and those related to brokers. The table given below gives the details of investors' grievances that have been received by SEBI since its inception and their redressal rate. Constant follow up and deterrent actions have helped in redressing an increasing proportion of investors' grievances. The large number of complaints received clearly indicates the inadequacies of the existing systems and practices in Indian securities markets. These grievances are also a reflection of the rising expectations of investors from intermediaries in the securities markets. The intermediaries in the primary and secondary markets such as brokers, sub-brokers, underwriters, merchant bankers, bankers to the issue, share transfer agents, and registrars to the issue are required to be registered with SEBI. The increasing number of investors' grievances indicates that investors' satisfaction and investors' confidence area set to become central issues in the development of securities market in India.

TABLE XVII

Investors' Complaints Received by SEBI

Year	Complaints Received	Complaints Resolved	Redressal Rate
1990-1991	18,794	4,061	22%
1991-1992	1,10,317	22,946	21%
1992-1993	3,51,837	66,308	19%
1993-1994	5,84,662	3,39,517	58%

Source: Indian Securities Markets, Agenda for Development and Reforms, p.10.

It is evident from the above table, that the redressal rate is only 58% in the year 1994 and it strongly suggest that there should be an active role of investors' service organisation besides the SEBI. In this context, it is worth to mention the services rendered by some of the investors' service centres like Integrated Enterprises in the private sector in Tamilnadu State.

Effectiveness of Investors' Services

One of the constituents of the present reform strategy has been the investors' services rendered by Integrated Enterprises, Madras. Following table clearly indicates the services rendered by the Integrated Enterprises to the investors to take precautionary measures while investing in corporate securities.

Table XVIII
Investors' Grievances - Causes & Solutions

Sl. No.	Kind of Grievance	Causes	Solutions
01.	Non-receipt of refund order/ share certificate against application lodged.	1. Misplacement of application by bank and hence non-receipt of application by the registrar for processing. 2. Data entry error in the name and address/ mismatch of address on the computer. 3. Losses in postal transit. 4. Skipping of refund orders at the time of computer overprinting due to lack of control at the Registrar's end. 5. Refund instruments being withheld for want of further clarification/reconciliation with the bankers. 6. Application's address not being mentioned in the application form or the same not being written legibly.	For the first one month after dispatch, one should reply giving the details of refund order/ share certificate, to the investor. Should the investor write once again in this regard, the Registrar will then forward a proforma of an indemnity bond so as to enable him/her to execute the same.
02.	Name of investor spelt wrongly, a wrong name being printed or name not being printed at all.	1. Error in data entry of the name and overlapping the same at the stage of verification. 2. Applicant not writing his name legibly. 3. Misprinting on the computer system due to power fluctuation.	Fresh refund orders are typed out and issued to investors immediately on receipt of investor's communication.

TABLE XVIII (Contd.)

Sl. No.	Kind of Grievance	Causes	Solutions
03.	Refund order torn/defaced/ MICR (Magnetic Ink Code Reader) code not existing.	1. Magnetic ink code reader not being printed is due to error at the print-end which happens in large volume refunds. 2. Refund orders are torn partially while tearing and inserting the instruments into envelopes. 3. Instruments get torn/ defaced in postal transit.	Fresh refund instruments are issued immedi-ately on receipt of the defaced instruments from the investors.
04.	Excess/short re-funds	1. The share consultancy services take the amount against each application as has been mentioned in the bank schedule whenever there is a variation between the amount mentioned in the application form and the bank schedule. In case a higher amount is shown in the bank schedule then the higher amount is taken, but the refund order is withheld. This is due to the fact that the company has received funds only as per the bank schedule.	In case, the investor provides details of the entry in his pass book or a bank certificate to the effect then a supplementary refund order is issued to the investor first, and follow up actions initiated with the bankers. In case no evidence is produced then the investor is forwarded copy of the bank schedule wherein his application is listed. A letter is also written to the concerned bank to explain variations and refund the excess money, if any, to the investor con-cerned directly.

TABLE XVIII (Contd.)

Sl. No.	Kind of Grievance	Causes	Solutions
05.	Delay in replying to investors with regard to status of their applications.	1. The investor would not have mentioned his application number in his letter or has not mentioned the correct number. 2. Investors application number does not appear in the registers maintained by registrar/ the company either due to a data error or otherwise. 3. There is a difference in application number on the application form and the counter foil. 4. No application number has been printed on the application form. 5. Registrar's inefficiency being overburdened. 6. Non-receipt of letter at the registrar's end or misplacement of investors letter. 7. Investor's letter crossing despatches of the refund orders/share certificates in transit. 8. Records being transferred to the company immediately after being processed, and hence no records being available at the registrar's end to be in a position to reply.	In cases, where the authorised consultancy agency are not in a position to locate the application number, one should write to the investor requesting him to get in touch with the bank where the application was lodged and obtain the bank serial number under which the application was listed in their schedule.

TABLE XVIII (Contd.)

Sl. No.	Kind of Grievance	Causes	Solutions
06.	Delays in transfers	1. Documents being received belatedly by the registrars for processing. 2. Registrars not receiving confirmation of the payment of allotment money from the bankers. 3. Companies not holding transfer committee meetings regularly. 4. Funds not being provided for despatch by the company or deliberate intent of the company to delay despatch of transferred documents.	This is a very serious problem that is being addressed to investors' services undertaking by the investors and the possibilities are being explored to ensure that transfers are processed and despatched on a weekly basis. There has been a significant improvement with regard to transfer Company Law Board's action penalising various companies recently.
07.	Documents not transferred	1. There have been certain cases where companies maintain separate sets of registers with different agencies. For example, records pertaining to an intial public issue of an existing company may be maintained by the company itself whereas records pertaining to a new issue of either equity shares or debentures are maintained by a separate external agency. The process of consolidation of record is in certain cases, delayed considerably and in the interregnum the certificates/ other securities, pertaining to the old issue and the new issue that are lodged for transfer are processed separately. This results in the investor being confused with regard to the total status of the documents submitted by him, since he will be receiving one set of documents of one time and the other set subsequently.	Split location processing puts the investors into considerable inconvenience. This also puts a considerable strain on the authorised agency since records are maintained at two different places and they do not exercise total control. The situation in all these cases has to be corrected and clients should be advised that transfers should be centralised at one place.

TABLE XVIII (Contd.)

Sl. No.	Kind of Grievance	Causes	Solutions
08.	Share certificates not refunded in time after endorsement	1. The authorised share consultancy/company will have to await confirmation of the payment of allotment money from the collecting bankers before endorsement of the share certificates, While this process normally takes 45 days after the last date specified for payment, in a period of the banking system being heavily loaded with public issues, this is relegated to the background by them and the details are forwarded sometimes, after 2/3 months from the last date	The authorised share consultancy or the company normally send an acknowledgment that the investors documents have been received at our end for endorsement in case on immediate endorsement is not possible. In order to overcome the problem nonreceipt of information from the banks due to the extension of last dates for payment of allotment money by the company, investors' services organisation have now initiated a process with the collecting banks to forward interim statements along with counterfoils to the investors' services undertaking so that delays are reduced to the maximum extent possible.
		2. Delays are compounded sometimes by the company's action to arbitrarily keep extending the last date specified for payment of the allotment money. In one case payment of allotment money the first, second and final call money was extended on three separate occasions for a total period of two and a half months. The fact that the last date has been extended is only notified through newspapers and many of the investors may not be having the relevant information. In such cases, endorsement of the share certificates is delayed.	

TABLE XVIII (Contd.)

Sl. No.	Kind of Grievance	Causes	Solutions
09.	Delay in issue of Duplicate refund orders	As already mentioned above, duplicate refunds are to be issued immediately on receipt of indemnity bonds from the investors. However, in the case of a few foreign banks acting as refund bankers, the banks lay down stipulations that the duplicate refunds should not be issued irrespective of obtaining indemnities till reconciliation normally takes a period of 150 days from the date of issue of the refunds i.e. 60 days after validity of the period of the refund order. This results in unmitigated harassment of investors who have not received their refund. Further, in certain cases, issues of duplicate refunds after reconciliation is also retained with the refund bankers and this process itself takes about 15 days from the date of forwarding the statement by the registrars. All in all, the existing process makes the investors suffer considerably and results in a delay of atleast 5 months by the time the investor receives his duplicate refund.	All issue's should be intimated that during the validity of the refund instruments duplicate refund instruments should be issued to investors upon receipt of necessary indemnities from them. Further, in case of large volumes or high value refunds, a certificate from the investors bankers can be obtained that the proceeds of the refund have not been credited to his account. In order to cut short the delays, the registrars should stipulate in their letter of offer itself that the client should make adequate provisions for issue of duplicate refunds without inconveniencing the investors irrespective of the refund being completed.

TABLE XVIII (Contd.)

Sl. No.	Kind of Grievance	Causes	Solutions
10.	Complaints arising out of deficiencies in designing of instruments/ devising procedures.	The reasons vary from instrument and the most comman examples are as under: 1. The company promising to effect payment of interest on application money, allotment and call monies received from the date of realisation of the cheque/ payment of cash without making any provisions for intimating of such dates by the collecting bankers. The collecting bankers in most cases do not have the dates and hence this results more often than not the commitment not being fulfilled. 2. Issuing a single letter of allotment for the total quantum of shares/ debentures applied for instead of forwarding a notice for payment of allotment money together with share certificate/ debentures letter of allotment in market lots. This results in the investor being unable to sell the negotiable instruments upon allotment. He will have to necessarily obtain a split document from the company before effecting any sale . 3. Complicated nature of instruments issued by a company, especially with varying quantum of payments makes cross checking on the computer system impossible and results in a greater number.	The only remedy will be for the registrars to be involved in the exercise at the time of devising the instrument and their advice being taken seriously before the instrument is devised. It has been out experience that even the most investor friendly companies sometimes devise instrument at a very high level of sophistication which cannot be under-stood completely by the common investor. Additional incentives such as effecting payment of interest more often than not result only in protracted correspondence since the existing system does not provide for full particulars being made available to the registrars. It is suggested to be involved in the exercise of finalisation and devising the instruments.

TABLE XVIII (Contd.)

Sl. No.	Kind of Grievance	Causes	Solutions
		4. Companies issuing simultaneous notices for payment of allotment money, call money where the total amount against an instrument to be received in parts. 5. Devising an instrument in a manner which will result in the converted instruments not being in market lots.	
11.	Non-receipt of interest/ dividend warrants on time	1. Substantial transfers being received at the time of book closure. 2. Company not being in a position to arrange requisite funds. 3. Company deliberately delaying release of payment by not providing adequate funds for postage.	So far as the process of transfers is concerned, stock exchange member have now devised the procedure of effecting transfers on a daily basis at the time of book closures. Necessarily provisions are being made for on-line updation also so that delays are eliminated. Investors services organisation also proposed to bring it to the notice of SEBI/ Stock Exchange in the event of delays occuring in effective payment of interest, dividend due to deliberate actions of the client companies.

TABLE XVIII (Contd.)

Sl. No.	Kind of Grievance	Causes	Solutions
12.	Delays in allotment	1. Bankers not handling over applications within the stipulated time. 2. Huge response being received. 3. Application being misplaced in transit. 4. Reconciliation of application money not being completed by the bankers. 5. Inadequate infrastructural facilities with Registras.	One of the remedies provided in the Companies Act is for payment of interest in case of delay in despatch of refunds. The most important reason as to why delays occur is due to belated receipt of applications from the collecting bankers. With SEBI proposing to issue detailed guidelines, investors' services organisation hope that this is obviated.
13.	Delays in receipt of stockinvests	1. The procedure with regard to stockinvests initially provided for the cancelled instruments being sent to the bankers. 2. For the successful applications also, the time taken for obtaining credit of the investors account was substantial since it had to pass from the company to the bank to the issuing bank and then the respective bank branch.	The procedure with regard to return of stockinvest has now been modified by SEBI and so far as cancelled stockinvests are concerned. In fact, most of the investors are now receiving the stockinvests atleast a week prior to despatch of regular refunds. The procedure with regard to acceptance of valid stockinvest instruments for encashment is still in the process of being streamlined, and investors will have to bear for atleast some more time.

TABLE XVIII (Contd.)

Sl. No.	Kind of Grievance	Causes	Solutions
14.	Correspondence arising out of rejections made due to improper utilisation of stockinvests	1. Investors utilising stock invests issued out of two or more application in contravention of the guidelines issued by SEBI in this behalf. 2. A number of investors failed to sign the stockinvest instruments while forwarding the same, along with the application. There have also been a number of instances of the branch manager not signing the stockinvests. 3. The stockinvest account number is not mentioned on the instrument issued by the banker.	In all these cases, the investor suffers due to his application accompanying stockinvests in such a manner being rejected. The complaint levels from investors in this regard are substantially high. A process of educating investors is required, so that investors understand the procedures to be followed for utilisation of stockinvest instruments. This is of a recent origin and is likely to create considerable amount of confusion in the minds of investors if not attended to immediately.

Source: Integrated News, Integrated Enterprises, Nov' 94, p. 14.

Summary

It is essential from the point of view of promoting investors' confidence in their investment, to create a sound investment environment which needs redressing the grievances of the investors. In this regard, the services rendered by Sebi to redress the grievances of investors' are worth to mention. However, in view of growing capital market activities, besides SEBI, investors' service centres in the private sector should also come out in large number to redress the grievances of investing community.

References

1. The chartered Accountant, Institute of Chartered Accountants of India, New Delhi, September 1993.

9

Summary of Findings, Suggestions and Conclusion

I. Background of the Study

The increased growth of investors, the proliferating investment opportunities, the changed economic policies and the new investment environment have necessitated investors' protection. In India, in the context of share markets witnessed of stock market scam, it is now clear that there must be a closer regulation of share markets and thereby giving protection to the investors become necessary in various legislations. In this connection, a study has been undertaken to examine the ongoing trading activities both in primary market and secondary market in India. Even though specialized protective agencies such as Securities Exchange Board of India (SEBI), Company Law Board (CLB) and stock exchanges are in existence for investors' protection, it is considered that still they have to go a long way. The present study has been carried out with the main aim of examining the need for investors, protection, the effectiveness (or) otherwise of the statutory provisions incorporated in the Companies Act, 1956, Securities Contracts (Regulation) Act, 1956, and SEBI Act, 1992 dealing with the trading activities in the primary and secondary market, and the adequacies (or) otherwise of the legal provisions in these three statutes dealing with investors' protection.

To make the study more practical, an opinion poll was conducted (through interview schedule) among the 100 respondents, namely, (stock brokers, professionals and investors). A specially structured interview schedule was administered for the collection of respondents' views on primary and secondary market trading practices in India. A fund of secondary data was mobilized from the leading magazines in India and abroad to furnish a mine of materials required for the present study.

From the discussion made in the previous chapters of this report, the major findings of the study are given in the following passages:-

II. Major Finding's of The Study

1. As the individual investor community and the investment avenues like investment in equity shares, preference shares, bonds, mutual funds are on the rise, it is interesting to know how the investors should be protected through various legislations. Even though there are various opportunities available of investment, investors' are scared of investing in companies. In this situation, the investors' protection becomes highly essential. In this regard, it is worthwhile to mention the effectiveness of the legislations namely Companies Act, 1956, Securities Contract (Regulation) Act, 1956, SEBI Act, 1992 meant for investors protection.
2. The object of the Company Law is to provide for an effective protection to the investors, creditors and public at large. Company Law Board, Registrar of Companies are the authorities under the Companies Act, 1956. It is found that the growth of public limited companies depends on the inflow of equity funds, which cannot be sustained unless the equity holders are taken care of. Today, in India, the problems of investors' who are outside the controlling group, are manifold without any effective remedy. When the prospective equity holders lodge their applications for shares, they are at the mercy of the companies. The present study has examined these problem which are summarised below:

(a) Non receipt or delay in receipt of refund orders, stock invest cheques, allotment letters, share certificates, dividend warrants, annual reports, confirmation letters for change of address and the like.

(b) Delay in effecting transfer of shares and return of share certificates.

(c) Non-receipt or delay in receipt of bonus shares/rights application forms.

(d) Inability to participate in shareholders meetings and voice their views on bonus or rights issue proposals or to raise queries on accounts, auditors' comments, company's operation and the like.

(e) Inability to prosecute company or its directors or officers for violation of company law or other legislations.

(f) Inability to influence the decisions of controlling group on appointment of directors, auditors and others.

It is found that the Central Government has overall responsibility for thc administration of the Act. The administration is sent through the Department of Company Affairs. The authorities under that Act are Company Law Board and Registrar of Companies. The legal provisions meant for the investors' protection are mentioned below:

Legal Provisions Meant for Investor' Protection

Sec 59– deals with penalty for error in the issue of prospectus.

Sec. 62– has to do with civil liabilities for misstatement in the prospectus.

Sec 63– spells out criminal liability for the misstatement in the prospectus.

Sec 68– deals with penalty for fraudulently inducing persons to invest. (In the above cases, Department of Company affairs has to take action.)

Secs 73, 73 (2A), 73 (2B)– interest on delayed refund and penalty against defaulting companies.

Secs 73 (1A), 73 (2)– for listing of the securities of the company to be granted permission within 10 weeks of closing of subscription list.

Secs 58 (A), 58 (4) (9) 58 (A) (10)– repayment of deposits in accordance with terms and conditions and right to approach Company Law Board.

Sec 84– issue of duplicate share certificates.

Secs 113, 113 (2)– Company in normal circumstances delivers share/debenture certificates within 3 months of allotment with fine of Rs. 500 for every day of default.

Secs 111, 111 (2), 111(3) 111 (4)– Company to register transfer and deliver share/debenture certificates within 3 months of allotment with fine of Rs. 500 for every day of default.

The study brings to limelight the lapses existing in the provisions of the Companies Act, 1956 meant for investors' protection:

(a) Reliance Consultancy Services issued duplicate shares to Ms Rajul Vasa and her family members of the Reliance group without obtaining indemnity bond, thereby it has violated Section 84 of the Companies Act, 1956.

(b) In another case, Reliance Consultancy Services issued duplicate share certificates to Oriental Insurance Corporation of India without giving public notice. Again there is a violation of sec. 84 of the Companies Act, 1956.

3. It is to be noted that the trading activities in the primary market are mainly governed by the legal provisions of SEBI Act, 1992. In this context, it is worth to mention the objective of SEBI (i) The SEBI was established as a statutory body on February 21, 1992. The main object of SEBI is to regulate the business in stock exchange and

to protect the interests of investors in securities. In order to ascertain the views of the respondents' on primary and secondary market trading, the researcher has contacted 25 brokers and 25 investors and 50 professionals in Madras city. The analysis of the responses has made following revelations:

A. Primary Market

I. A majority of respondents' namely, stock brokers, investors' and professionals consider that following are the factors affect the primary market trading at present in India.

(i) Pricing of premium issues.

(ii) Inadequate disclosure of information in prospectus by issuing companies.

(iii) Overpricing of right issues.

II. In order to ascertain the degree of concord in the respondents' views on the factors affecting primary market trading activities, the respondents' are divided into two groups, namely, one group consisting of brokers, and another group comprising of investors' and professionals. The stock brokers consider that the following factors affect the primary market trading at present in India.

(i) Pricing of premium issues.

(ii) Delay in allotment of shares and issue of certificates and

(iii) Inadequate disclosure of information by issuing companies.

The investors' and professionals expressed that the following factors affect the primary market trading,

(i) Pricing of premium issues.

(ii) Overpricing of right issues, and

(iii) Inadequate disclosure of information by issuing companies.

It is found that the views expressed by two groups of respondents' (stock brokers and investors/professionals) over one factor namely, delay in allotment and issue of certificates, slightly differ.

III. In regard to their age, the respondents' under different age groups consider the factors affecting primary market trading practices differently. To illustrate, respondents who are in the age group of below 35 years consider the following factors affect the primary market trading,

(i) Pricing of premium issues.

(ii) Delay in allotment of shares and issue of share certificates, and

(iii) Differential pricing of promoters' and inadequate disclosure of information by issuing companies.

The respondents' who are in the age group of 35-50 years consider the following factors affect the primary market trading,

(i) Pricing of premium issues.

(ii) Overpricing of right issues, and

(iii) Inadequate disclosure of information by issuing companies.

The respondents' in the age group of 50-65 years consider the following factors affect the primary market trading,

(i) Overpricing of right issues.

(ii) Ineffective handling of issues by brokers.

It is found that the views expressed by the respondents' in the different age groups consider differently on the factors namely, Ineffective handling of issues by brokers.

IV. In regard to their income, the respondents' under different income groups consider the factors affecting primary market trading differently.

Respondents' falling under the monthly income of below Rs. 5,000 consider that the following factors affect the primary market trading: –

(i) Pricing of premium issues.

(ii) Inadequate disclosure of information by issuing companies, and

(iii) Differential pricing of promoters.

The study participants in the income groups of Rs. 5,000 - Rs. 10,000 and Rs. 10,000 - Rs. 20,000 consider the following factor affect the primary market trading,

(i) Pricing of premium issues.

The respondents in the income group of above Rs.20,000 consider the following factors affect the primary market trading.

(i) Delay in allotment of shares and issue of share certificates.

(ii) Overpricing of right issues.

It is found that the views expressed by the three groups of respondents, over one factor namely, delay in allotment of shares and issue of share certificates which affects the trading activities in the primary market.

V. In regard to the views of the respondents on primary market trading based on professional qualification wise, trading and investment status wise, there is a similarity of opinion between the groups of respondents' namely, professionally qualified and not professionally qualified, often traded and often not traded, invested and not invested consider that the primary market factors like pricing of premium issues and over pricing of right issues does not affect trading activities in the primary market.

Concerning the trading activities in the primary market, survey data has made the following disclosures: -

(i) Pricing of premium issues.

(ii) Delay in allotment of shares in the issue of share certificates.

(iii) Overpricing of right issues.

(iv) Inadequate disclosure of information by the issuing companies.

are the major factors affect the primary market trading at present in India. It indicates that in order to safeguard the interest of investors, primary market operation are to be regulated.

B. Secondary Market

The analysis of survey data concerning the factors affecting secondary market trading are furnished here under: (It is to be noted that the trading activities in the secondary market are mainly governed by the legal provisions of SEBI Act, 1992).

I. The majority of the respondents' consider that the operation of modified badla system, pessimism and lack of confidence, delay in settlement of cash transactions are the factors responsible for the sluggish secondary market trading practices.

II. In order to ascertain the respondents' views on the factors affecting secondary market trading, the respondents' are divided into two groups, namely, one group consisting of stock brokers and another group comprising of investors' and professionals. The stock broker consider that following factor affects the trading activities in the secondary market at present in India.

(i) operation of modified badla system.

The investors' and professionals expressed that the following factors are responsible for the secondary market trading.

(i) operation of modified badla system.

(ii) Delay in settlement of cash transactions, and

(iii) Lack of and slow movement of funds.

It is found that the views expressed by the two groups of respondents' (stock brokers and professionals/investors) vary with the two factors namely, delay in settlement of cash transactions, and lack of and slow movement of funds which affect the trading activities in the secondary market.

III. In regard to their age, respondents' under different age groups consider the factors affecting secondary market trading activities differently. To illustrate, respondents who are in the age group of below 35 years consider the following factors affect the secondary market trading,

(i) Pessimism and lack of confidence among investors.

(ii) operation of modified badla system.

(iii) Mutual fund operation.

(iv) Lack of and slow movement of funds .

The respondents' who are in the age group of 35-50 years consider the following factors responsible for the secondary market trading,

(i) operation of modified badla system.

(ii) Delay in settlement of cash transactions.

(iii) Restrictive regulations.

The respondents' in the age group of 50-65 years consider the following factors responsible for the secondary market trading,

(i) Pessimism and lack of confidence among the investors.

(ii) operation of modified badla system.

(iii) Lack of and slow movement of funds, and

(iv) Mutual fund operation.

It is found that the views expressed by respondents' in the different age groups are differently on the factors, namely, delay in settlement of cash transaction and restrictive regulations, that affect the trading activities in the secondary market.

IV. In regard to their income, the respondents' under different income groups consider the factors affecting for the secondary market trading differently. To illustrate, the respondents' falling under the monthly income of below Rs. 5,000 consider that the following factors responsible for the secondary market trading:-

(i) operation of modified badla system.

(ii) Pessimism and lack of confidence among investors, and

(iii) Slackness in regulations.

The study participants in the monthly income groups of Rs. 5,000 - Rs. 10,000 and Rs. 10,000 - Rs 20,000 consider the following factors responsible for the secondary market trading,

(i) Operation of modified badla system.

(ii) Delay in settlement of cash transactions.

(iii) Mutual fund operation.

The respondents in the income group of above Rs. 20,000 consider the following factors responsible for the secondary market trading,

(i) Slackness in regulations.

(ii) Mutual fund operation.

(iii) Lack of and slow movement of funds.

It is found that the views expressed by the respondents' in the different monthly income groups consider differently on the factors, namely slackness in regulations, operation of modified badla system, pessimism and lack of confidence among investors, and lack of and slow movement of funds affecting the activities in the secondary market.

V. In regard to the views of the respondents' on secondary market trading based on professional qualification wise, trading and investment status wise, there is a similarity of opinion among these groups of respondents, namely, professionally qualified and not professionally qualified, often traded and often not traded, invested and not invested consider that the secondary market factors like operation of modified badla system, mutual fund operation does not affect secondary market trading at present in India.

Concerning trading activities in the secondary market, survey data has made the following disclosures:

(i) Operation of modified badla system.

(ii) Delay in settlement of cash transactions.

(iii) Pessimism and lack of confidence of among investors are

(iv) Slackness in regulations.

are the major factors affecting the trading activities in secondary market at present in India.

C. Insider Trading

An attempt was made during the survey to analyse the views of stock brokers, professionals and investors' on the practice of insider trading. Questions arranged in the form of statements and the responses recorded on a five point scale. The main findings are:

(i) The stock brokers, investors' and professionals consider that insider trading is a regular feature and it occurs on certain specific occasions like the issue of shares and convertible debentures of listed companies. They have agreed that it is harmful to the market and it provides undue advantage to certain traders over others.

(ii) Most of them have disagreed with the statement that the present regulatory mechanism is adequate to control the insider trading. The respondents' clearly hold the view that SEBI's insider trading regulations are inadequate to prevent and control insider trading in Indian stock markets.

(iii) In regard to the views of the respondents' on insider trading based on their age, income, professional qualification and trading status in the market, they also consider that SEBI's insider trading regulations are rather inadequate to prevent and control insider trading in Indian stock markets.

D. Pricing of Securities

The analysis of the responses of the views of sample stock brokers, investors' and professionals on the pricing of securities has made the following revelations:

(i) A majority of the respondents have agreed that the method of pricing of premium issues is fair and acceptable and strongly agreed that the justification for the fixation of pricing of premium method is vague and inadequate.

(ii) The respondents in the different age groups, monthly income groups, professionally qualified and not qualified and often traded and often not traded agree that it is possible to influence the price of a security by unfair means.

E. Operation of Modified Badla System

The survey indicated the views of the sample stock brokers, investors' and professionals on the operation of modified badla system. The major findings of the study in this regard are:-

(i) A majority of 60% of the respondents consider that the operation of modified badla system is harmful to the market and it should be banned.

(ii) Forty per cent of the respondents' have agreed that the operation of modified badla system helps in stabilising the market. However, they support that effective regulations are requried for the operation of modified badla system as the existing SEBI regulations on the operation of modified badla system are inadequate.

(iii) The respondents' in the different age groups, monthly income groups, professionally qualified and not qualified, often traded and often not traded, have also agreed that effective regulations are required for the badla system as the existing SEBI regulations on operation of modified badla system are inadequate.

F. Futures and Options

The survey indicated the views of the sample stock brokers, investors and professionals on the operation of futures and options. The major findings of the study in this regard are:

(i) A majority of the respondents have agreed that the futures and options system provides better alternative to the modified badla system, and therefore, they consider, there is no need to delay and exercise caution in introducing this system of futures and options.

(ii) The respondents' in the different age groups, monthly income groups, professionally qualified and not qualified, often traded and often not traded, have also agreed that futures and options system provides better alternative to the operation of modified badla system and SEBI regulations for the futures and options are essential.

G. Investors' Protection Measures

The survey indicated the views of the sample stock brokers, investors' and professionals on investors' protection measures. The major findings of the study in this regard are:

(i) A majority of the respondents have agreed that investors' have adequate opportunity for participation in security investment.

(ii) The respondents' in the different age groups, monthly income groups, professionally qualified and not qualified, often traded and often not traded, have agreed that SEBI investors' protection measures have to be considered seriously for the protection of investors in the market.

4. It is essential from the point of view of promoting investors' confidence in their investment to create a sound investment environment which needs redressing the grievances of the investors. In this regard, the services rendered by SEBI to redress the grievances of investors' are worth to mention. However, in view of growing capital market activities, besides SEBI, investors' service centres in private sector should also come out in adequate number to redress the grievances of investing community.

III. Suggestions for Investors' Protection

As examined in detail in the preceding chapters of present research report, since, investors are the backbone of growth of capital market, need for investors' protection is of paramount importance. While designing the statutory measures meant for investors' protection, the following suggestions deserve immediate attention.

1. COMPANIES ACT, 1956

(a) Review of abridged prospectus is essential for investors' protection. It should contain the salient features of the complete prospectus. The lead manager or merchant banker may be required to include in his 'due diligence' certificate, a paragraph to the effect that the abridged version fairly sets out all the features of the complete prospectus .

(b) The Sachar Committee's recommendations such as right to speak and the right to vote on show of hands to be extended to proxy holders shall be included in the new Company Law Bill.

(c) Stringent conditions have to be made when the companies decide to enter the capital markets. For this purpose Company Law Board should have more powers to punish the companies for violating the provisions of the Companies Act, 1956.

(d) As there is a lapse in the existing Companies Act, 1956 with regard to the issue of duplicate share certificates (as pointed in Chapter III of the present research report), necessary amendments should be made in the Companies Act in the provisions dealing with the allotment of shares to the public and issue of duplicate share certificate.

2. SEBI Act, 1992

(a) The changing economic scenario, the major economic reforms and liberalization measures initiated by the central government such as globalisation of Indian capital market all these will present enormous opportunities to the private and public sector companies to tap their requirements of resources. For this purpose, the SEBI should be given more powers to regulate the capital market.

(b) In order to safeguard the interest of the investors, strict regulations should be made in the primary market operation such as pricing of premium issues, allotment of shares, adequate disclosure of information by the issuing companies and so forth.

(c) SEBI should be given more powers to supervise effectively the secondary market operation like insider trading, operation of modified badla system, futures and options in order to safeguard the interests of the investors.

(d) It is necessary for SEBI to take action against erring management of the companies, so that investors' complaints against the issues or dealings in securities can be dealt with promptly and satisfactorily. In this connection, investors' grievances centre (as branches of SEBI) may be opened through out India for speedy redressal.

(e) SEBI has not paid attention to take action against unauthorized share trading houses for dealing in corporate securities. The illegal operation of these trading houses and their exploitation of investors need to be looked into and regulated. Here , it is worth to point out (the inadequacy of SEBI's function in relation to M.S. Shoes Company's affairs as mentioned in the chapter V of the present report.)

(f) SEBI should also try to establish a cadre of top executives for manning higher level post in the stock exchanges. There is a dearth of trained, experienced and suitable personnel for the post of Executive Directors, and SEBI has to attend to this matter urgently.

(g) SEBI's guidelines are silent on the functioning of the market intermediaries when they break the rules on the issue of corporate securities. As a part of solution, three specific measures have to be taken to protect the investors, namely,

(i) Rating of market intermediaries

(ii) Introduction of boughtout issues, and

(iii) Scribbles trading.

3. Investors' Services Center

In view of growing capital market activities, besides SEBI's investors grievance center, investors' service center should also come out in required numbers to redress the grievances of investing community. Such centers, vested with appropriate powers, may be established, to look with sympathy and understanding the investors' problems. These centers may have the mandate to take effective and prompt actions, and also have an exclusive jurisdiction to deal with the woes of the investors.

IV. Conclusion

At present in India, three different statutes, namely, Companies Act, 1956, Securities Contracts (Regulation) Act, 1956, and SEBI Act, 1992 regulate the trading activities in the stock markets both primary and secondary. The irregularities (or) limitations found in the primary market operation are in the pricing of premium issues as well as inadequate disclosure of information in the prospectus and over pricing of rights issues. The irregularities (or) limitations are also found in secondary market operation which are in the operation of modified 'Badla' system, as well as pessimism and lack of confidence among investors and the delay in the settlement of cash transactions. These irregularities (or) limitations found in the primary and secondary market trading activities could well be corrected by conferring the SEBI with more powers as in the line of suggestion made in the present report. The Present study has brought to sharp focus that there is slackness in the regulatory provisions in the two statutes, namely Companies Act, 1956 and SEBI Act, 1992, especially in the legal provisions pertaining to the issue of duplicate share certificate and SEBI's guidelines for the issue of shares. The procedural lapses in these statutes must be corrected as suggested in this research report. Further, as suggested in the present report, the investors' service centres in the private sector may come up in adequate number (to redress the grievances of the investors) in order to supplement the functioning of investors' grievance cell of the SEBI.

❑ ❑ ❑

Index

D

E

F

G

I

J

K

L

M

N

O

P

R